fluff

fluff

THE STICKY SWEET STORY OF AN
AMERICAN ICON

MIMI GRANEY

BOSTON

UNION PARK
PRESS

Union Park Press
P.O. Box 81435
Wellesley, MA 02481

Printed in the U.S.A.
First Edition

Library of Congress Cataloging-in-Publication Data
Names: Graney, Mimi, author.
Title: Fluff : the sticky sweet story of an American icon / Mimi Graney.
Description: First edition. | Boston : Union Park Press, [2017] | Includes
   bibliographical references and index.
Identifiers: LCCN 2016054274 | ISBN 9781934598191 (alk. paper)
Subjects: LCSH: Marshmallow--United States--History. | Candy industry--United
   States--History. | Durkee-Mower, Inc.--History.
Classification: LCC TX791 .G774 2017 | DDC 641.85/30973--dc23
LC record available at https://lccn.loc.gov/2016054274

Book and cover design by Holly Gordon Perez
www.valehillcreative.com

Inside front cover: First row, left to right: (c) Union Square Main Streets, Kraft advertisement, Courtesy Durkee-Mower, Courtesy Boston Public Library. Second row, left to right: Mars advertisement, Domino advertisement, Courtesy Durkee-Mower, Lowney's advertisement. Third row, left to right: First National Stores label, Lowney's advertisement, Courtesy Boston Public Library. Fourth row, left to right: Courtesy Durkee-Mower, Baby Ruth advertisement, First National advertisement.

Inside back cover: First row, left to right: Reed Candy Company advertisement, Courtesy Boston Public Library, Courtesy Durkee-Mower. Second row, left to right: Lowney's advertisement, Courtesy Durkee-Mower, Lowney's advertisement. Third row, left to right: Courtesy Boston Public Library, Curtiss Candy Company advertisement, Courtesy Durkee-Mower, Kraft advertisement. Fourth row: Courtesy Durkee-Mower.

Page vi: Courtesy Durkee-Mower.

UNION PARK
PRESS

unionparkpress.com
KEEPING BOOKS IN STYLE SINCE 2007

To the man who makes my life super sweet, Scott R. Loring

Recommend
MARSHMALLOW
fluff

for Plum Pudding Sauce

A NEW *Way*
to use

MARSHMALLOW
FLUFF

Delicious Home Made
ICE CREAM

CONTENTS

Courtesy Union Square Main Streets.

INTRODUCTION

AT the dawn of the twenty-first century, the city of Somerville, Massachusetts was inching toward renaissance. The population of this tough, working-class community was slowly evolving. Alongside blue collar Irish and Italian families who had raised their families here, new waves of immigrants were arriving from Brazil, Haiti, and Central America. Students and young professionals who had once fled to tonier neighborhoods the minute they could afford to do so were now staying put, calling Somerville home.

The little-used factories that had provided jobs for the city's residents decades ago were now becoming petri dishes of reinvention, waking up one by one. Painters, sculptors, and jewelers converted the former cannery and bakery for A&P stores into live-work condos. The unused floors of the Rogers Foam Corporation on Vernon Street became art studios. Rock bands and circus performers rehearsed at the former complex of American Tube Works.

Davis Square, on the west side of Somerville, was on the rise—thanks in large measure to a new public transit station—but Union Square, on the east side of the city, remained mostly unchanged. A century before, Union Square was the dynamic downtown of Somerville, with a hotel, theaters, and every sort of retail establishment. Streetcars stopped there over one hundred times a day, ferrying in commuters and shoppers. But the same decline that felled cities across America in the 1950s and 1960s hit this neighborhood particularly hard. Despite local efforts, it had yet to recover. Burdened by traffic and trash, vacancies and vagrants, Union Square remained stagnant.

To turn things around, a group of neighborhood stakeholders came together to form a non-profit organization called Union Square Main Streets (USMS) and I was hired to head it up. Following a national model for grassroots economic development, we brought together the entire community—business owners, residents, government workers, and property owners—to create a shared vision for a more prosperous future. The Somerville Arts Council, a department of the City of Somerville, was a key partner to USMS. With exemplary creative leadership and a track record of community-based projects, the Arts Council had just been awarded a multi-year grant from the Massachusetts Cultural Council to enact an arts-based economic revitalization program called ArtsUnion.

Within the ArtsUnion initiative was a series of weekend mini-festivals, each proposed and produced by a different community partner. I took responsibility for the very first event, organizing a celebration to mark the inauguration of the new Union Square Farmers Market in 2005. It was delightful: The "Queen of the Garden Vegetables" arrived, wearing a twenty-four-*carrot* necklace. There was a parade with stilt walkers from the nearby kids' circus camp, a face painter, and live music. Through the course of that first year, each successive happening topped the last, demonstrating more and more imagination and cleverness: Showcases featuring local choreographers, celebrations of Brazilian, Latin American, and Indian culture, and the most unique miniature golf course you can imagine, with holes designed and fabricated by local artists. One highlight of that season was when Project MUM (Meet Under McGrath) transformed the litter-strewn, heavily pigeon-pooped spot under the McGrath highway overpass into a neighborhood dance club with DJs, light installations, and go-go dancers. By the end of the year, we were drawing several hundred people to each of these events.

For the second year, however, I wanted an event that would capture this growing energy and tell the story of Union Square itself. In conversations on how we might advance the neighborhood, many pointed toward Kendall Square—just two miles south in Cambridge, but a world away. This high-profile hub was booming with world-changing biotech and internet innovators. Angel investors roamed the corridors of slick offices, seeking the Next Hot Thing. "You should make Union Square more like Kendall Square," I was told more than a few times, but that struck me as a fool's errand. Truth was, I didn't share their aspirations. I loved Union Square and Somerville exactly as it was, with its scrappy, eccentric charm, finding soulful beauty and life on these dusty streets. If others were introduced to the Somerville I could see, I was sure they'd fall in love too.

Union Square resident Mike Katz playing the role of Archibald Query at the annual Fluff Festival. *Courtesy Union Square Main Streets.*

I was also a long-time collector of Somerville-related trivia, and I'd noticed that whenever I mentioned Marshmallow Fluff was invented in the city, I received an animated response. No other product provokes such feelings of fond reminiscence and passionate loyalty among New Englanders than Marshmallow Fluff. Like Vegemite for Australians, haggis for the Scots, and mom's kimchi for Koreans, Fluff inspires an affection that is often beyond comprehension to those who aren't in the know.

My second festival concept was an attempt to bottle (or jar) that energy. The idea was a wink at all those enthusiasts of "innovation" and Somerville's chronic position as second banana to Cambridge. The 2006 result was a madcap event to honor Marshmallow Fluff and its inventor, Archibald Query. We called it "What the Fluff? A Tribute to Union Square Invention."

My most optimistic hope was to draw four hundred people to the event. But well over a thousand showed up on the Union Square Plaza for that first Fluff Festival. There was music, "science" contests, Fluff-inspired games, a cooking contest that attracted both the delicious and the ridiculous (an erupting Fluff volcano!), plus the requisite Fluffernutters. As the festivities came to a crescendo with an impromptu tug-of-war over a pool of the sweet, white confection itself, it was exceedingly clear that we had struck a cultural chord.

Since 2006, the festival has become enshrined as a New England tradition, held the last Saturday of each September. As the silliness caught the attention of the media, Marshmallow Fluff devotees arrived from near and far, swelling attendance to over ten thousand. Despite the crowds, the event remains a gathering of the diverse Somerville community in wholesome, sticky-sweet play. The food vendors, made up of small, locally owned businesses and community groups, incorporate Fluff into their products, adding it to everything from ice cream to pizza to cocktails to empanadas. The games remain free, Fluff-themed, and decidedly DIY. (Think: Fluff Bowling, Fluff Jousting, and Fluff Musical Chairs.)

Through the festival's popularity, Somerville—and Union Square in particular—have become synonymous with Fluff. The Victorian-era Prospect Hill Monument overlooking the neighborhood once served as a civic symbol, but today the motif is more likely to be a jar of Marshmallow Fluff. There are no apparent misgivings among the city's officials. In fact, when Mayor Joseph Curtatone exchanged gifts with the leader of Somerville's sister city, Tiznit, Morocco, Tiznit offered up an ornate ceremonial necklace of silver and fine stones; Somerville presented Tiznit with a jar of our favorite marshmallow cream. Fluff has become so closely identified with Somerville that many don't know that, aside from a brief time before World War I, it was (and still is) manufactured by the Durkee-Mower Company a few towns over in the City of Lynn.

Since that first Fluff Festival the fortunes of Union Square have shifted dramatically. New restaurants, cafés, and shops are lauded for their excellence. A new light rail line is under construction to return public transit to the area. The markers of sustained disinvestment, like the scrap iron yard and waste transfer station, are gone. A master developer from Chicago was selected by the City to complete $1 billion in new construction, promising high-rises and high-tech for dear old Union

Square. While I'm not claiming that Marshmallow Fluff was the secret ingredient, there is something magical that happened because of that silly, sticky spread. You might only think of Fluff as an ingredient for sweet sandwiches and folksy desserts, but to my mind, it has also proved to be a powerful tool to reinvigorate, enliven, and ultimately help transform a languishing city.

For many Somervillians, the changes are dizzying and inspire more than a tinge of worry. What will become of the local character we adore? How do we address the rising rents that are beginning to displace the current residents and businesses that call Union Square home? How do we understand our neighborhood identity when development is leading us toward our long-time foil Kendall Square? How to navigate such challenging times?

✦

Marshmallow Fluff was born during Union Square's first boom a century ago; and over the years, against the odds, it has remained true to itself. It is easy to celebrate Fluff without learning its history—it's deliciously weird—but to know the whole story is to understand how an unusual,

Flufferettes strut their stuff at the *What the Fluff?* festival in 2010.
Photo by Geoff Hargadon.

Photos courtesy Durkee-Mower.

utterly American foodstuff has both survived and thrived through the decades. As odd as it sounds, Fluff's longevity could have the answers for how Union Square and other business districts might navigate change.

Marshmallow Fluff is just a whipped concoction of four commonplace ingredients. And, as its very name implies, it seems little more than a trifle. I had no idea what I would uncover when I set out to learn everything about Marshmallow Fluff and the company that produces it. The story turned out to be far bigger and more fascinating than I ever imagined. Through the lens of a simple, somewhat whimsical product such as Fluff, we learn about the history of food production, trade and commerce, the media, gender roles, and so much more. In the one hundred year history of one small business we discover how the same forces shaping its narrative are more broadly reflected across America's cities and towns. By understanding Durkee-Mower's recipe for success, we learn the essential roles of buoyant innovation, ambitious creativity, and steadfast, sometimes cantankerous, tenacity. Exploring this simple product opens a complex story about our country, the American zeal for progress and innovation, and how icons are made.

fluff IN HISTORY

1764
First U.S. commercial production of chocolate begins, establishing Boston as a candy-making center.

1812
Corn syrup is invented by Russian chemist Gottlieb Kirchhoff.

1853
The Boston Sugar Refinery develops white granulated sugar.

18TH CENTURY

19TH CENTURY

1920
Durkee-Mower company forms on Valentine's Day, starts making "Toot Sweet Marshmallow Fluff" and hard candies.

1922
WNAC radio opens in Shepard's Department Store in Boston.

1940
Durkee-Mower switches from tin to the "liberty glass jar."

Durkee-Mower sells 4 million cans of Fluff in New England, making it the best-selling brand of marshmallow cream.

1926
First major advertising campaign by Durkee-Mower launches with premier of the Flufferettes on WNAC radio and series of print ads in the *Boston Post*.

1939
Germany invades Poland.

1941
Japan bombs Pearl Harbor.

2006
Somerville hosts the first *What the Fluff?* festival.

2000
Durkee-Mower produces 7 million pounds of Fluff with 20 employees.

21ST CENTURY

2007
Fluffernutters, introduced by New England-born astronauts Sunita Williams and Richard Linnehan, become a popular treat on the International Space Station.

2017
Marshmallow Fluff celebrates its centenary.

1857
Dover Stamping and Manufacturing Company in Cambridge, Massachusetts invents the hand-operated eggbeater.

1906
Pure Food and Drug Act prohibits misbranded and adulterated foods, drinks, and drugs in interstate commerce.

1910
Limbert Brothers launches its "Marshmallow Fluff."

1896
First reference to marshmallow crème appears in a recipe by Boston-based cook and educator Fannie Farmer.

20ᵀᴴ CENTURY

1917
Archibald Query invents Marshmallow Fluff.

United States declares war against Germany.

1919
Great Molasses Flood hits Commercial Street in Boston.

Fred Mower and Archibald Query meet while working together at Lowney's Chocolate Company.

1918
Germany surrenders on November 11.

1947
Commercial sugar rationing is lifted.

Fluff is sold in every state east of the Mississippi River.

1949
Durkee-Mower's new factory on Empire Street opens, capable of producing 5,000 cases of Fluff per day.

1950
Durkee-Mower celebrates its anniversary with a grand opening of the factory.

1966
Durkee-Mower partners with Kellogg's to promote Rice Krispie Treats.

1958

The Fluffernutter is named. Fluff distribution reaches 70 percent of the United States.

Factory employees wrap chocolate bars, circa early 1900s.
Courtesy Library of Congress.

NECCO workers on the line, 1928. *Courtesy New England Confectionery Company.*

The Cradle of
American Confections

NEW ENGLAND had a sweet tooth long before Marshmallow Fluff entered the scene, and chocolate was its first love. In Europe, drinking chocolate was a luxury, served in elegant pots and dishes with all the sophistication befitting such an exotic, exclusive beverage. In the New World, however, cacao was more affordable because of direct trade routes from the West Indies and freedom from tariffs, guilds, and controlling monopolies. Easy access turned drinking chocolate into a daily eighteenth-century ritual; families roasted and ground the cacao beans, mixed them with water or milk, and then sweetened the resulting drink with imported sugar, domestic honey, or maple syrup. Like Europeans, Americans also ascribed to chocolate a variety of medicinal benefits, such as aiding digestion, curing headaches and depression, and restoring strength to the ailing.

It was in Boston in 1764 that the first commercial production of chocolate in America began. Irish chocolatier John Hannon had learned commercial-scale chocolate making in London, a craft not yet mastered outside of Europe. Once settled in Boston, he met American-born physician and grocer James Baker. Valuing the health benefits and medicinal uses of chocolate—as well as the business opportunity—Baker financed Hannon's lease of a water-powered gristmill to grind their first cacao beans. They launched their company on the Neponset River in what is now Dorchester and called it the Walter Baker Company.

Not long after Hannon and Baker set up shop, other entrepreneurs throughout the region enlisted mills to manufacture chocolate, most notably in Central Falls, Rhode Island, where William Wheat's mill on the Blackstone River gave the town the nickname Chocolateville.

Just a decade after commercial production of Baker's Chocolate began, drinking chocolate saw a significant spike in popularity. In the wake of the Boston Tea Party and other protests against British tea taxes, revolutionaries across the colonies, particularly in Massachusetts, deemed drinking tea unpatriotic. Drinking chocolate provided a delicious (and passive aggressive) alternative. This chocolate binge came to an abrupt halt, however, when blockades during the Revolutionary War limited all imports, including cacao and sugar.

By the time regular trade was restored in the early 1780s, American attitudes toward chocolate had changed. After years of strife on both sides of the Atlantic, with Americans freeing themselves from the reign of a British King and the French ousting their own aristocracy, all things connoting nobility had soured in popular consciousness. Though it had been a populist beverage on this side of the Atlantic, the European association between elitism and drinking chocolate affected American tastes too, and it fell out of favor.

But it was delicious—and purportedly nutritious and medicinal—so chocolate could never completely lose its appeal. In the early 1800s, chocolate bars became the favored conveyance. The Walter Baker Company developed bars that were less prone to spoiling and sold them wrapped in wax paper with a money-back guarantee of freshness.

These blocks of chocolate—dense, portable, and packed with calories for quick energy—became America's first fast food. Whalers off the coast of Massachusetts stashed them in their pockets for sustenance and shared them on their travels. Prospectors carried them west to California during the Gold Rush of the 1800s.

As their product traveled from coast to coast, the Walter Baker Company emerged as a national brand. By the dawn of the twentieth century, the company had nine hundred workers and a complex of grand, industrial buildings forming the centerpiece of Dorchester's

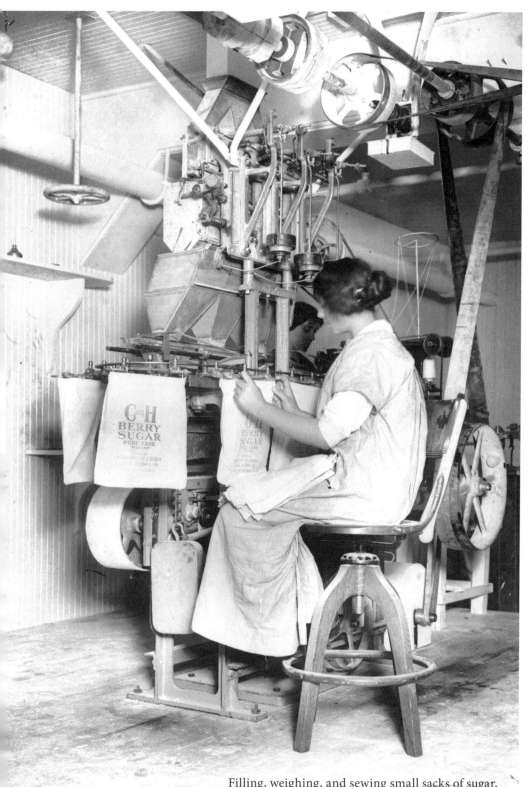

Filling, weighing, and sewing small sacks of sugar, circa early 1920s. *Courtesy Library of Congress.*

Lower Mills area. This attracted clusters of small businesses and homes meant to serve the factory's workers, giving the neighborhood the nickname of the Chocolate Village.

✦

Before climate-controlled facilities, hot days meant melting cocoa butter and rancid product. New England's cool climate gave chocolate makers—and the generations of confectioners to come—an edge over southern states hoping to break into the game. Even in relatively temperate Boston, chocolate making was initially a seasonal activity reserved for the cooler months. Despite these hiatuses, Boston emerged as the national leader in confections. It was a position the city held well into the first part of the twentieth century, in no small part because of its strong transportation network; raw ingredients of sugar, molasses, cacao, and vanilla were brought in by sea, and the finished sweets were distributed across the city's thriving rail system.

An industry was born. Two sugar refineries, one in East Boston and another in nearby Revere, converted raw sugar into its edible components. A large workforce—some of them European immigrants familiar with candy making and many others willing to learn—built and labored in the fast-growing factories that dotted the region. Industrial investors and innovators enabled this early generation of confectioners to grow quickly.

Chocolate wasn't the only sweet staple in the region; before the advent of candy stores, apothecaries mixed sugar (also considered medicinal) with other remedies to make more palatable lozenges and sugar drops. Befitting the era, these types of makers were small, neighborhood businesses. In the 1800s in Salem, Massachusetts, the company known today as Ye Olde Pepper Companie began by making Gibralters, a combination of sugar and peppermint oil, and then Black Jack, made with blackstrap molasses. Black Jack became the nation's first commercially sold stick candy. The confections traveled widely, carried by the area's seafaring merchants around the globe, but the candy's identity remained tied to its place of manufacture, as Salem Gibralters and Black Jacks were local institutions. The scale of manufacture was small and the tools—cooking pots and common utensils like spoons, knives, and scissors—were simple.

As the Industrial Revolution advanced in the second half of the nineteenth century, however, forward-thinking entrepreneurs and inventors entered the candy scene. Boston's Oliver Chase mechanized the manufacture of confections when he created the lozenge cutter machine in 1847. Chase's invention, comparable to a pasta maker, produced flat, round disks of a consistent size and thickness. Chase's lozenges were sold to soothe dry throats and settle upset stomachs, and they quickly developed a following under the name of Hub Wafers. With his brothers Silas and Daniel, Chase built a company on those lozenges along with their popular Conversation Hearts, multicolored heart-shaped candies with romantic inscriptions. Eventually, the Chase venture merged with three other candy companies to become the New England Confectionery Company, known today as NECCO.

NECCO wafers—like other candy of the period—were considered a valuable, non-perishable food source, and as such achieved an odd, iconic status. NECCO wafers were brought along on two major expeditions: Donald MacMillan's trip to the Arctic in 1913 and Admiral Richard Byrd's voyage to the South Pole in the 1930s. Byrd packed two and a half tons of NECCO wafers for his trip, an allowance of a pound a week for each of his men on the two-year voyage. This unofficial endorsement, coupled with dozens of other successful products, helped grow NECCO into one of the world's largest candy companies. In Cambridge, Massachusetts, NECCO anchored "Confectioner's Row" amid a cluster of other candy manufacturers, including Daggett Chocolate, George Close Company, Squirrel Brand Company, Nabisco, James O. Welch Company, and Fox Cross Company.

Building on the concept of the lozenge cutter, a huge variety of small tabletop machines emerged in the second half of the 1800s to improve efficiency and decrease the need for skilled labor. With whimsical, Wonka-like names such as the Kiss Knocker, the Champion Candy Crimper, the Cut Drop, the Stick Candy Spinning Machine, and the Humbug, confectioners were now able to quickly cut and consistently form hard candies into specific shapes. Powered by hand cranks and utilizing rollers, cutting wheels, and assorted dies, pliable sugar ropes or slabs were fed through one side of the machines as uniform pieces emerged from the other.

Perhaps the most important innovation for confectioners was the revolving steam pan, developed in Philadelphia in 1843. This machine used steam to both cook candy and power the moving parts of the factory. Instead of manually stirring open kettles of chocolate and boiling sugar, the revolving steam pan agitated the liquid and kept it from burning. The mechanization of this dangerous, exhausting task mitigated the risk of injury and allowed factories to operate with fewer workers and mix larger, more consistent batches.

For soft, chewy candy, the candy press—developed in the mid-1800s—enabled the quick creation of marshmallows, gumdrops, fondant, and gel-centered candies like jellybeans. By 1899, the candy press was automated and transformed by a new invention: the starch mogul. This clever improvement was an enclosed box inside which wooden trays were filled with starch, compressed flat, then indented with a set of desired shapes. Those trays of starch were then used as molds, with the candy liquid poured into the cavities. Once the candy solidified, the trays were flipped over to release the gooey treats. Marshmallows were ready to eat, while other candies like jellybeans and gumdrops received an additional sugar or chocolate coating. The leftover starch would be sifted and reused for the next batch.

The starch mogul also vastly improved factory safety. The starch room in any candy factory was a dangerous place, as the airborne particles were prone to explode. The enclosed container of the mogul limited

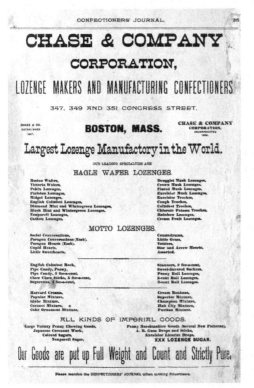

Chase & Company advertisement, January 1890. *Courtesy Library of Congress.*

the starch released into the room, reducing that risk. Modern confectioners still use starch moguls, albeit with some updates, of course.

Shortly after the development of the starch mogul, the enrober changed the game for traditional chocolatiers. Invented in France in 1902, the enrober eliminated the labor-intensive task of hand-dipping chocolates. Bonbons, caramels, cookies, and other treats were placed on a screen and passed on a conveyor belt through a steady stream of chocolate. Rollers underneath coated the bottoms. The results were attractive, almost as pretty as hand-dipped chocolates, though the coating wasn't quite as thick—a benefit for confectioners seeking to economize on cocoa.

The Schrafft Candy Company, founded in Boston in 1861, used the starch mogul and enrober to grow its business, specializing in the large-scale manufacture of gumdrops and boxed chocolates. By 1928, the company was operating the largest candy factory in the world on the Charlestown side of Sullivan Square. With sixteen hundred workers in that plant alone, Schrafft's produced a wide range of treats, including candy canes, candy corn, spearmint leaves, cakes, and ice cream.

In a move that would impress today's venture capitalists, Schrafft's expanded its business to include the operation of motor lodges along the length of the East Coast and fifty-five restaurants, mostly in New York. Those restaurants, which have been called the "mid-century restaurant version of Starbucks," were high volume, moderately upscale, distinctly urban, and ubiquitous.

Schrafft Candy Company advertisement, circa 1950s.

✦

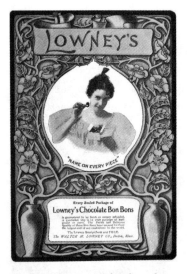

Walter M. Lowney's Chocolate
Bon Bons Candy advertisement
in *Good Housekeeping*, 1904.

At the turn of the twentieth century, Schrafft's had one local rival: the Walter M. Lowney Company. After a childhood spent in Maine, Walter Lowney learned about the manufacture of confections in Philadelphia, another major candy-making hub. Lowney moved to Boston and began making caramels. By 1886, Lowney's candy dippers were turning out one ton of choice chocolates a day from a single factory on Pearl Street in Boston. Even without the use of a chocolate enrober, Lowney's sold four million packages of bonbons in 1899.

With that kind of output, Lowney's company needed all the production space it could muster. In 1905 Lowney was operating two factories in Boston, one on Pearl Street and another on Commercial Street, as well as a massive plant in Mansfield, Massachusetts, with two hundred thousand square feet dedicated to production. He also had another large facility in Montreal, Canada. For distribution, the company maintained numerous retail outlets and offices throughout northeastern United States and Canada.

The growth of the Walter M. Lowney Company was felt most markedly in the town of Mansfield. Just as Hershey, Pennsylvania developed around the Hershey Chocolate Company's factories and the benevolence of its founder, Milton Snavely Hershey, Mansfield, Massachusetts fulfilled the vision of Walter Lowney and his company. Drawn to the town by the available land and proximity to the railroad, he built his fourteen-acre complex on Oakland Street in 1903. At the company's peak, he employed one thousand Mansfield workers in a monumental six-story building.

Lowney developed the town of Mansfield to meet his company's needs. He financed the town's water and sewer systems. Across the street from the factory, Lowney Farm's dairy cows provided the milk for the factory's milk chocolate. He created housing for his workers, many of them recent Italian immigrants, in ten duplexes nicknamed "Lowney Houses." He guided the development of municipal infrastructure, donating land for the Town Common (now known as North Common), and encouraged the creation of a town manager position to facilitate local government. Since there wasn't a place to host out-of-town visitors and social gatherings, he built a popular hotel and restaurant in the town center called The Tavern, living there himself for a period. He established the Lowney Airfield where, in 1925, a freelance pilot landed on the grass runway and gave sightseeing rides for a dollar. He constructed a baseball field and sponsored the home team. His patronage went all the way down to the grassroots with donations to the Mansfield Boys Club.

The company's most popular early product was Lowney's Cocoa, marketed as a breakfast beverage. But it was Lowney's bonbons that became the company's mainstay. These memorable treats were packaged in fancy, reusable tins emblazoned with effusive slogans like, "Gateway to the Good Graces of those who love the Good Things of Life."

✦

Though the treats they produced were sweet, life in a candy factory was less so. For confectionery workers, the biggest dangers were explosions, respiratory illnesses, and burns. Airborne sugar, cocoa, and starch are highly combustible and presented a daily threat. The development of the starch mogul helped lessen the hazard caused by that ingredient, but the other light, powdery particles remained a concern. After emptying bags and barrels of ingredients into open kettles, workers would be coated from head to toe, the air cloudy with particles. Because factories lacked air filtration systems, workers commonly suffered from lung ailments. Both the steam to power the machines and the large pots of sticky, molten sugar could do serious harm as well.

By way of compensation, confectionery jobs—at least those with the largest companies like Lowney's—often came with attractive benefits such as pensions, paid time off, and life insurance. Some employers like New England Confectionery made medical care available with a doctor

These teenage boys worked as coconut shavers in the Kibbe's Candy Factory, Springfield, MA, October 1910. *Courtesy Library of Congress.*

and nurse on site for workers and their families. The Walter Baker Company offered sick leave and shortened workweeks.

Lowney, however, took the wellbeing of his workers a step further. Starting in 1907, workweeks were limited to forty-seven and a half hours. All of Lowney's employees received annual bonuses as part of a profit-sharing program. Demonstrative of the company's success, the profit-sharing pot was $15,000 in 1906 and grew to $24,000 in 1908—more than half a million dollars today. In 1914, any employee who had worked for the company for at least a year received what a contemporary trade association called a "substantial sum of money," along with a note from President Walter M. Lowney: "We are sensible of the fact that our success has come only through united effort and we believe such effort should have reward and recognition that it may always continue."

In Mansfield, all this bounty was the envy of nearby communities. (Residents of Foxborough mocked the community, calling it Lowney-town.) If there were any misgivings in Mansfield about Lowney's largess, folks kept it to themselves. All reports were that Walter Lowney was held in universally high regard.

For the likes of Lowney's, Schrafft's, and other major confectioners, the Industrial Revolution and the resulting inventions were major labor savers. What had previously taken a full day of cutting boiled sugar for hard candies like lemon drops and humbugs now only took fifteen minutes. The starch mogul alone slashed the task of fifteen workers down to three.

These technological advances also removed the skill required for many traditional candy-making tasks, so while the number of workers in candy factories grew in the first decades of the twentieth century these were primarily lower wage, unskilled jobs. Chocolate dipping had been mainly women's work that could garner a wage of nine dollars a week. Using the enrobing machine meant that the task was downgraded to loading and unloading the belts of product entering and leaving the machine. What had once been a skilled trade, now automated, required no specific knowledge or expertise. Meanwhile, as candy making became increasingly proprietary, companies began to guard their recipes more closely. Company owners kept ingredient sources and production details secret from even their own employees. By the 1930s, those tasked with making candy were no longer artisans or craftspeople holding specialized skills or technical knowledge. For the tens of thousands working in confections the tasks were now rote.

With dramatic increases in production and steep reductions in the need for skilled labor, candy making emerged as a highly profitable business with explosive growth. In 1850, there were 383 factories and 1,733 workers producing $3 million worth of confectionery nationwide. By 1900, that had grown more than tenfold, with just shy of 4,300 factories and 33,000 workers producing $60 million worth of candy each year. A decade later, production doubled, with annual revenues exceeding $135 million, and it continued to grow exponentially. By the mid-1940s, candy was America's $1 billion industry.

fluff

CONFECTIONERY FACTORIES LIKE LOWNEY'S—a true giant among Boston's confectioners—provided employment opportunities to women and talented candy dippers; piece-work, in particular, generated significant income. To entice applicants in 1920, a large display advertisement ran across the *Boston Globe's* Help Wanted section, featuring the chatty Nellie Walsh of the Personnel Department:

Dear Folks:

There is a lot more than mere work in being in the employ of the Walter M. Lowney Company.

I am going to tell you about some of the things we do here.

In the first place, of course, we employ a large number of girls and women, and many have been here for years.

They like their work, and that is a big advantage for them. They are contented and happy.

We are taking on new people all the time, and right now we are looking for a lot. …

Did you know that the Boston Health Department made the usual thorough inspection a while ago and gave us a rating of 100%? That is a pretty good showing.

The work is interesting and agreeable, and is the kind that make you feel as though you had accomplished something when the day is all done. You can picture some fellow taking a box of Lowney's Chocolates to his girl and you have an interest in helping him out and doing your best with the box. …

Did you ever hear about our L.C.A.—That is the Lowney Cooperative Association. Everyone belongs.

The L.C.A. has to do with all things like Cafeteria, Mutual Benefit,

Store, Credit Union, Legal Aid, etc.

The Legal Aid has been a benefit to many of the people because it has helped them in their own personal troubles when they didn't know just what to do.

There are classes in Dancing and Millinery, and sometimes a show—there are a lot of people here who can do stunts. Then we have movies noons where we can all sit down in the dining room and the change rests us for the afternoon's work. ...

There is a Rest Room with books to read and—of course, the nurses when we need them. ...

Fifty men from the Americanization Classes went up the other day and took out their "first papers." Wasn't that fine! They are so interested in the classes.

Come to the Battery Street Elevated Station, walk down to 486 Hanover Street, take elevator to the fourth floor, Personnel Department, and ask for me. I'll be there.

Nellie Walsh

P.S. Read my fifth paragraph again.

A photo of Miss Nellie Walsh with this brief biography accompanied the letter:

Some time in the early [18]90s Miss Nellie Walsh came to Lowney's to work in the Bonbon Department during her school vacation. She found the work so congenial and everybody so pleasant and friendly that she soon became a regular member of the Lowney family. She has steadily risen until today she is in the Personnel Department interviewing our girls interested in Lowney's.

fluff

✦

It wasn't just technology that impacted the candy business. World War I dramatically affected the price and availability of sugar and cocoa, the key ingredients in any confection. Sugar was needed for armaments, as molasses was converted into industrial alcohol and its chemical components used to make explosives. Demand for sugar spiked across the globe at the start of World War I as surplus stores were quickly depleted. European sugar beets were unavailable as the fields were etched with trenches for battle instead of furrows for crops. Meanwhile, major agricultural producers of sugarcane were unable to effectively respond—like the Philippines, hobbled by drought and an epidemic. Ships were available and freight costs were low, but without access to the raw materials sugar prices skyrocketed. In 1919, the cost of sugar was double that of the previous year.

To meet the world's demand, sugar production in the United States surged dramatically. The United States exported 2.5 million tons of refined sugar during World War I, sourcing the raw material from cane grown in Cuba and Louisiana and domestically grown sugar beets. The leap was massive: two and a half times more sugar was produced in the United States in those three years than in the preceding forty-five years combined.

Along with its use in armaments, the military relied on sugar to provide a portable source of quick calories for the troops. While once considered a battlefield luxury, candy was an essential part of World War I combat rations. Early on, the American military was buying 150 tons of candy each month, and the amount grew steadily as the war carried on.

In earlier conflicts, chewing tobacco had been the go-to salve for soldiers. During World War I, however, American soldier turned to candy—hard candies, chocolate, and especially chewing gum. Chewing gum, which activates the salivary glands, served as a substitute for water for troops on the march, and with food sometimes in short supply, it helped quell hunger. Battlefront dental care was likely low on the list of priorities for the individual soldier, but the military understood that poor oral hygiene could be the army's undoing in the long term. The military encouraged gum as a preventive to tooth decay and deemed it a positive alternative to chewing tobacco. How popular was chewing gum? In just the month of February in 1919, Wrigley's alone shipped 3.2 million packages of gum to meet its share of a government order.

The federal War Industries Board (WIB) set production quotas for confections, priorities for distribution, and uniform prices that the military would pay to ensure adequate supplies. The prices set by the WIB enabled manufacturers to earn higher-than-market profits on their military contracts. This created a powerful incentive for the major suppliers to ramp up production. For these special orders, companies typically produced unique items to help the war effort. The Walter Baker Company, for example, produced chocolate bars for World War I troop rations under a new W.T.W. brand—the initials standing for "Win the War." These sales gave a major boost to the largest candy manufacturers and a great advantage over smaller confectioners after the war.

With the military claiming such a giant share of sugar and cocoa, stateside supplies were limited and prices were highly volatile. Smaller American candy makers needed to get creative if they were to remain in business. One solution was shrinking the sizes of individual candy pieces. Packages of sugar wafers and chocolate bars were reshaped, slimmed, and miniaturized, all in an attempt to keep the same consumer price while allowing the confectioner to maintain a profit. Another way to limit the use of sugar and chocolate without reducing the size of the bar was to mix in cheaper, more accessible ingredients. Raisins and other dried fruits added sweetness and bulk without sugar. Gooey fruit centers could fill out a product while still meeting consumer interests. Ingredients like coconut, oats, popcorn, and puffed rice and wheat were cheap and added appealing flavor and texture. Companies selling these ingredients marketed themselves to confectioners with the promise of "the old-time size at the old-time price." Sweeteners that were more readily available, like corn syrup, presented yet another option. Confectioners developed recipes for nougat, caramels, and marshmallow that enlisted this substitute. This economic necessity bred innovation, and confectioners quickly birthed a whole new breed of concoctions that would become the modern candy bar.

Lowney faced the challenge by developing the Cric Croc and the Milk Chocolate Crispy bar; both used puffed grains to stretch the chocolate further. Chocolate-covered raisins, dates, and nut milk bars were quickly added to the lineup. Lowney developed complex candy bars too,

fluff

The Squirrel Brand Company factory. *Courtesy of the Cambridge Historical Society, Hollis G. Gerris Collection [3.271]. Cambridge, MA.*

including the That's Mine (with the slogan of "Six Inches of Dandy Candy"), the Caravan (a bar of chocolate-covered marshmallow and caramel), the Milk-Nut-Loaf ("A Good Bit for Five Cents"), and the Eat More peanut chew. A few of Lowney's creations are still around, including the Cherry Blossom, which remains a cult favorite in Canada. The Cherry Blossom is an oversized maraschino cherry in juicy cherry fondant, coated with a mixture of chocolate, roasted peanuts, and coconut.

Before World War I, candies were named by descriptors: sour drops, bonbons, caramels. But these new concoctions were given singular, more fanciful names to set them apart and drive sales. Confectioners played on popular trends by using names of celebrities and national crazes, and some of those specially named treats are still available in the candy aisle today. Massachusetts-based confectioner Fox Cross Company took a bar of flavored nougat, covered it with chocolate, gave it the name of the latest dance craze, and launched the Charleston Chew. The Squirrel Brand Company developed the Squirrel Nut Zipper, a vanilla-nut caramel. In the former home of Paul Revere in Boston's North End, the Charles N. Miller Company introduced the Mary Jane bar, a chewy molasses-and-peanut butter candy.

America emerged from the war with a whole new relationship with sweets. In 1919, when the military's overwhelming need for sugar abated, the federal Sugar Equalization Board suspended US exports so that confectioners could better meet the domestic clamor for all those hard candies, gums, jellies, caramels, and newfangled candy bars. America's production of sugar and candy continued even after the military urgency was gone. Candy was now ubiquitous. In 1900, per capita candy consumption was two pounds per year. In 1923, after World War I, it had risen to fifteen pounds. Store-bought sweets were no longer a small luxury but an American staple.

✦

Boston's cooler climate and successful ice trade had given the region an edge in making temperature-sensitive confections, but after World War I, with the advent of mechanical air conditioning, that advantage was lost. Though they continued to be significant players in the boxed chocolates industry through most of the twentieth century, the majority of Boston's candy producers were unable to keep up and the city lost its overall confection dominance to the larger urban centers of New York, Philadelphia, and Chicago. In 1950, there were 140 confectionery companies in Boston and Cambridge with sales totaling $200 million a year. By the end of the century, however, the growth of international candy conglomerates Hershey and Mars had essentially wiped Boston's confectionery industry off the candy map.

Production of Baker's Chocolate ended in Boston in 1969. Baker's Chocolate is now produced in Delaware under the immense umbrella of Kraft Foods. The Schrafft's factory building in Charlestown still stands and its iconic sign remains a Boston landmark, but candy making there ended in the 1980s. Professional offices fill the floors where candy machines once rumbled. NECCO downscaled to smaller facilities in Revere, Massachusetts, where those lovable wafers are still made today. The tiny shop of Ye Olde Pepper Companie continues to operate from a storefront in Salem, Massachusetts, providing an authentic taste of yesteryear. While older residents can recall the aromas of chocolate and vanilla wafting through the streets and visits to the factory store for small treats, little remains from Boston's storied candy past. Because of bankruptcies, acquisitions, retirements, and closings, just a tiny handful of Boston's manufacturers of these sugary delights remain. One of those manufacturers is central to this particular story, of course: Durkee-Mower, the makers of Fluff.

Store delivery in Union Square, Somerville, August 1912. *Courtesy Library of Congress.*

A Secret Recipe

FOR an energetic young man like Archibald Query, Boston in 1900 was exhilarating. The newly constructed South Station provided a noble gateway for rail passengers arriving from the South Shore, New York, and Washington, D.C. Cultural centers like Symphony Hall, the Museum of Fine Arts, and the Boston Public Library had just opened, heralding the sophistication of this Hub of the Universe. Boston's wealthier residents, having transformed the Back Bay with their tony mansions, were pushing the city's boundaries southwest into the Fens, developing more neighborhoods with splendid homes and tree-lined streets. It was a grand age for Boston—stylish, cultured, cosmopolitan.

But Boston was also a growing immigrant city. Every day, waves of newcomers—many of them Italian and Irish—crowded into the already congested poor and working-class neighborhoods of the North and West Ends. Archibald was an immigrant, but he wasn't a newcomer. Nearly two decades prior, he had emigrated as a child from the town of Sorel in southwestern Quebec to the town of Franklin, thirty miles southwest of Boston.

Archibald found a place to live at 26 Springfield Street in Somerville, where two-family homes were springing up on former farmland. Somerville's location, abutting downtown Boston and tucked alongside

fluff

Cambridge, Somerville was ideal for the region's growing middle and working classes, providing easy access to Boston's job market, its political and commercial centers, and all its social and cultural offerings, with far fewer urban woes. Though Somerville's new residences were tightly packed, with houses often less than twenty feet apart, the new neighborhoods were pastoral compared to Boston's congestion. Busy streetcars shuttled commuters and shoppers into downtown Boston, a mere three miles away, and with ninety miles of fine streets, three miles of boulevards, three heavy rail lines, and a web of streetcars, there was no hyperbole when community boosters declared Somerville's "transportation facilities second to no city in the state."

Archibald was twenty-six years old when he moved to Somerville, and he shared an apartment with the other Query family men: his father James and two younger brothers, Henry and Armand. Archibald's youngest siblings, sisters Vallie Rose and Emily, remained behind in Franklin with their mother, Malvina, and paternal grandmother, Joviet.

All the Query men were short with dark hair, and Archibald's thick locks were notably unruly, a wild mop on his head. James Query, Archibald's father, was a photographer and a printer, and Archibald's brother, Armand, followed him into these fields. Henry worked as a confectioner with Archibald. As the eldest son, Archibald likely served as an apprentice to a nearby tradesman. W. S. Russell was a notable confectionery company just a block away from the Query home in Franklin, so it's very possible Archibald developed his candy-making skills there.

Family lore tells us that Archibald—known for his feisty nature and sarcastic bent—was making confections in his Somerville home and selling them in small batches to local merchants and to customers door-to-door. Before zoning codes defined residential, commercial, and industrial districts, it was common for workplaces to be tucked inside, behind, below, and between residences. Business and health regulations were limited in 1900 so little would have encumbered Archibald's enterprise.

We don't know how Archibald met the love of his life, Elizabeth Ryan. Maybe she answered when he knocked on her door with his assortment of hard candies, marshmallow cream, or other treats? Archibald's grandson offers another theory: Elizabeth, also known as Lizzy, worked for a local grocer and was responsible for purchasing the wholesale confections.

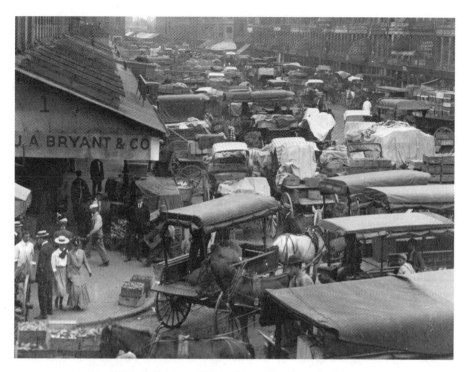

Faneuil Hall. Boston, 1906. *Courtesy Library of Congress.*

What we *do* know is that Archibald fell madly in love with a redheaded gal from East Cambridge. In July 1901, a justice of the peace married twenty-seven-year-old Archibald and twenty-year-old Elizabeth. Their marriage, which lasted more than sixty years, was particularly affectionate and produced two sons.

Archibald continued to make and sell his own confections, but maintaining a solo venture was increasingly difficult in the 1910s. Companies were growing bigger and were far better resourced than when he was starting out twenty years before. The fast-growing companies, producing and marketing on a much larger scale, easily outpaced a neighborhood-based business like Archibald's. While the confectionery industry did not demand the same bankroll as the steel and textile industries, small manufacturers needed better capitalization than a generation before if they were to remain at all competitive. The days of locally marketed, home-based manufacturing were fading quickly.

The final straw for many businesses like Archibald's came from the

Bird's eye view of Prospect Hill from Union Square Fire Station tower, 1923.
Courtesy Boston Public Library, Leslie Jones Collection.

taxman. Before 1913, nearly all small companies operated with the simplest of business structures. It was rare to incorporate and rarer still to obtain a business loan. Business owners were decidedly lax with their records, typically maintaining few, if any, accounts beyond individual customer reckonings. Documentation—when it existed—was informal, resembling personal journals filled with simple notes of daily activities and business details never intended to serve as public record. In 1913, however, the introduction of a federal income tax required businesses to establish proper accounting functions. These new formalities and sophistications made it less feasible and attractive for small operators like Archibald to continue.

Shuttering his small business was no reason for Archibald to leave the candy game, however. He had plenty of options nearby. The largest confectionery company in Somerville was Roy W. Carr, "manufacturing confectioner and wholesale dealer in Drake's chocolates," located at 601 Somerville Avenue, an easy walking distance from the Query house. Windsor Chocolates on Stone Avenue in Union Square was even closer. But the most enticing opportunity, one offering high pay and job security, was with Walter M. Lowney Company, Boston's chocolatier giant. Archibald's brother, Henry, found employment at the Lowney plant on Pearl Street while Archibald was a foreman at the Commercial Street plant.

It was while Archibald worked at Lowney's Boston factory that

World War I, the war that changed America's confectionery industry, began. At forty-three years old Archibald was too old to enlist but he nevertheless demonstrated his patriotism. Just three days after the United States declared war, and after thirty-seven years living in the United States as a Canadian, Archibald became a naturalized American citizen.

At the close of the war, Boston's candy industry emerged stronger than ever, producing and selling sweets of every sort for hungry American consumers. But other businesses predicated upon the industrial uses of sugar had emerged during this decade as well; namely the business of turning molasses into explosives. Peace was not going to be good for business. To survive, significant corporate shifts were needed. In this heartbeat before Prohibition, the production of booze was a viable alternative. It was during this juncture that Bostonians were exposed to the surprisingly disastrous results sugar could incur.

On January 15, 1919, at the Purity Distilling Company—just a block down Commercial Street from the Lowney plant where Archibald worked—the molasses tank, four stories tall and ninety feet wide, burst. The rivets broke away in a sharp "rat-a-tat-tat" and a towering, twenty-foot-high wave of 2.3 million gallons of thick, heavy molasses rushed through the streets. The force of the sugar wave wiped out the distillery and its offices, flattened all the nearby wooden structures, lifted stone and brick buildings from their foundations, and snapped the girders that supported the elevated train.

The *Boston Post* reported the surreal moment:

Molasses, waist deep, covered the street and swirled and bubbled about the wreckage ... Here and there struggled a form—whether it was animal or human being was impossible to tell. Only an upheaval, a thrashing about in the sticky mass, showed where any life was ... Horses died like so many flies on sticky fly-paper. The more they struggled, the deeper in the mess they were ensnared. Human beings—men and women—suffered likewise.

Rescuers stretched ladders across the goo in an attempt to reach those suffocating under the molasses. For four days, they continued to search for victims, setting up medical facilities in a building nearby to tend to the injured. All told, twenty-one people were killed and 150 were injured. Among the dead were a number of longshoremen and city workers from the nearby North End Paving Yard. Two local ten year olds were crushed by debris. The sixty-four-year-old woman who lived across the street was killed instantly when the wave demolished her home.

The property damage totaled $100 million in today's dollars. The mass of molasses destroyed everything in its path, moving south down Commercial Street all the way to the edge of Lowney's brick factory. In the aftermath of the explosion, the molasses remained knee-deep. More than three hundred people were enlisted for the public clean up. Chipping away at the mess in the winter cold, firefighters spent weeks pumping saltwater from the harbor to soften and blast away the hardened sugar. It took eighty-seven thousand man-hours to methodically wash the streets, sidewalks, and buildings, uncovering pieces of wreckage all along the way. The gutters and sewers dumped directly into the harbor where the dissolved molasses turned the water brown, a color it would remain until summer. Workers used sand to dry and cover the syrup, but wheels and shoes carried the stickiness throughout the city, down streets, onto streetcars, and into businesses and homes. As one newspaper reported, "Everything a Bostonian touched was sticky."

The Great Molasses Flood permanently altered the landscape of the city's waterfront and Commercial Street; those blocks were never rebuilt. (Today, the area is an open space, providing parks and a playing field for residents of Boston's North End.) Lowney's factory, just on the edge of the wreckage, continued to operate during the three-month cleanup—but there is no doubt operations were disrupted. Boston's North End was overrun with cleaning and repair crews, and residents were still reeling from this freak turn of events. The elevated train suffered significant damage and took longer to repair, making the commute to Lowney's all the more difficult.

Amid this chaos came a new flood: Hundreds of thousands of returning GIs walked the streets of Boston in search of work. Simultaneously, military contracts dried up and there were few opportunities for young men whose occupational skills were acquired on the battlefield. Securing a position at Lowney's factory—or anywhere for that matter—required persistence and charm. Fred Mower was such a fellow.

Aftermath of the 1919 Great Molasses Flood. *Courtesy Boston Public Library, Leslie Jones Collection.*

fluff

When Fred Mower was growing up in Swampscott, Massachusetts, life was relatively carefree. He had a group of close friends with whom he often engaged in low-stakes hijinks. At lunchtime, Fred (who was called "Dinty") and his friends Allen Durkee (nicknamed "Joe"), Walter Brennan, and Karl Frost could be found in the school's boiler room with the janitor, who entertained them with colorful tales of fighting in the American Civil War and his life as a fisherman. The boys debated the veracity of the old man's claim to have swum in the rough seas around Egg Rock with a lit cigar in his mouth, coming ashore as he puffed smoke.

They spent their Sundays playing instruments in the music shop owned by a friend's father. Allen and Walter played on the football team. Fred was into theater. When they could, they all got together to perform comedy skits and music at the Swampscott Club for a little extra cash.

Like many friendships born on the playground, they were poised to go their separate ways upon graduation. In 1915, Allen was off to the University of Maine where he joined the Sigma Chi fraternity and was part of the freshman football team. Fred followed his father and took a job operating a machine in a nearby shoe factory. Walter became a bank clerk. Karl enrolled at Boston University. But just twenty months after leaving high school, these Swampscott boys were reunited when they were called to serve their country in World War I.

Fred and Walter joined the army infantry and Allen planned to follow Karl into the navy. Allen had a particular love of sailing and considered the navy as a way to see the world by sea. He overslept the morning of his train from Bangor to Bar Harbor, however, and took this as a sign. His uncle was already in France, a colonel in the first contingent Canadian field artillery, and Fred and Walter had joined the twenty-sixth division of the 101st field artillery. Hoping to find familiar faces among the two million American men serving in France, Allen enlisted in the army and headed east. Not long after, Allen's younger brother Frank joined them on the battlefields of France as well.

Whatever romantic notions these young men had about war were quickly undone by nearly two grueling years in the trenches. They spent months standing in cold mud, the stench of death and rotting bodies filling the air, their nights sleepless amidst scurrying rats. They emerged from these horrors only to face the dangers of active battle.

Fred served in the supply company of the twenty-sixth division, while both Walter and Allen were in the expeditionary force of the field artillery. For part of the war, Allen was stationed in the 101st headquarters where he was a wireless operator. All three ended their tours with the rank of colonel.

The shared experience of war forged a powerful bond among the group that would last their whole lives. Safely returned home, they maintained regular communication and gathered formally with their brothers of the twenty-sixth division once a year, a tradition interrupted only when the next Great War overwhelmed their lives and took away their sons.

The battlefield left a common, indelible mark on Fred and Allen, as well as their close friends. Over the course of their lives, each demonstrated a willingness to take risks and a compelling drive to succeed, a sense of independence combined with a desire to collaborate, and a ferocious approach to work and play informed by the terrible paradox that life is at once tenderly precious and shockingly absurd.

Most of the men Fred and Allen grew up with entered the business world, either launching their own companies or successfully climbing the executive ladders of major corporations like Lever Brothers, Sylvania, and Noyes Buick. Karl joined his father's modest advertising agency and

World War I Artillery Division, circa 1917. Frank and Allen Durkee are in the back row, second and fourth from right, respectively. Fred Mower and Walter Brennan are in the middle row, second and fifth from left, respectively. *Courtesy Swampscott Historical Society.*

grew it into a regional player through contracts with several national brands. Of the friends, Walter Brennan achieved the most conspicuous success. Hurting for money, he reached back to those high school vaudeville days with Fred and tried his hand at acting. Walter's earliest parts found him beside another newcomer, John Wayne, and like the Duke, he launched a major career in movie westerns. Winner of three Academy Awards, he is widely regarded as one of the greats.

It wasn't all triumphant. For some, battlefield experiences were a burden that couldn't be overthrown. Frank struggled with the effects of mustard gas and trauma and was unable to find his place in the world. In July of 1947, police found him slumped over the steering wheel with a landscape sketch by his side. Public death notices said the cause of death was a heart attack, but his family believed it was suicide.

✦

Though the war officially ended in November 1918, it was the spring of 1919 when the men of Swampscott returned home. Archibald was a forty-six-year-old foreman and Fred Mower was a young man new to the world of confections. The Boston Harbor behind Lowney's factory was still brown from the Great Molasses Flood cleanup when they met on the factory floor that spring.

Despite their age difference, Fred and Archibald got along well. Both were gregarious and funny; Archibald was known for his sarcastic ribbing while Fred was known for a softer, silly sense of humor. Over breaks and lunch they met in the company cafeteria where Fred listened to Archibald's stories about his life in confections and learned about the sweet, tantalizing products Archibald had developed and peddled door-to-door before the war.

During the summer of 1919, Archibald and Fred worked together closely to organize the annual Lowney Company picnic. Archibald was in charge of the general arrangements, and Fred, playing to his strengths, managed the entertainment. While Lowney's "corporate culture" wasn't a complete anomaly—trade and social associations were robust in this period—Walter Lowney's commitment to worker welfare was notable. These friendly outings fostered an environment of camaraderie on the factory floor, which stuck with Fred.

Though the location of the annual Lowney outing changed year to year, the athletic program remained more or less the same. The traditional games provided the winners with a year's worth of bragging rights and a title to defend. Activities included a fifty-yard dash for women, a one-hundred-yard dash for men, and a sack race. In a tug-of-war match, the men of the bon-bon department took on the fellows from shipping, and then the women held their own contest. A baseball game pitted married men against their single counterparts. Other competitions had more bemusing names, like the Boys' Comedy Boxing, the Tonic Race, and "Hitting of the Cheese for Men." At the 1919 picnic, Walter Lowney himself presented prizes to the day's winners before Fred and his friends of the 101st Infantry Veterans Band provided entertainment to conclude the day.

Walter Lowney's Boston factory on Commercial Street. *Courtesy of Historic New England.*

✦

After the war, Allen Durkee went back to his parents' house in Swampscott. At twenty-three, Allen joked that he was too old to return to the University of Maine, but there was a ring of truth to it. Those innocent school days must have felt like a million years away. He'd spent the past months working as a carpenter, building homes alongside his father and pondering what he'd do next.

Allen must have been inspired by Fred's enthusiasm for the candy business, and he loved hearing the stories about Fred's coworker Archibald, the feisty French Canadian with the wild hair. That marshmallow cream Archibald used to sell door-to-door especially intrigued him. With some basic equipment, Archibald and his brother had whipped up the confection right in their own home.

Candy had been a good friend to them during those days on the battlefield: they chewed gum while on the march, sucked sweet hard candies to get them through the long nights on watch, and nothing was better than receiving a care package filled with homemade sweet treats. Confections could be their deliverance again. The muse Allen had been waiting for was here. They would make and sell that marshmallow cream.

The duo approached Archibald to acquire his recipe. It had been some time since Archibald had produced marshmallow cream for commercial sale and neither of his sons had shown any interest in confections whatsoever. He knew the value of his recipe, however, and it would take time to teach them the process, so in exchange for five hundred dollars (about six thousand dollars today) Archibald sold his recipe to Fred and Allen and instructed them in the manufacture of marshmallow cream. It was Valentine's Day in 1920 when the two friends celebrated the official opening of their business, simply called Durkee-Mower Company.[1]

✦

For the first couple months they worked from home, borrowed spaces, and enlisted friends to help. They felt their way into a business plan, trying out the manufacture of a few different sweets in addition to Archibald's marshmallow cream recipe. They tested some easy-to-make hard candies, particularly lollipops, but after evaluating openings in the market, potential returns, and merchandising strategies, they decided to abandon these. To increase their manufacturing scale, they knew they would have to focus on larger wholesale and business-to-business sales. To differentiate themselves in the increasingly crowded field of sweets, they narrowed their product line to supplies for bakers and other confectioners. They knew marshmallow cream would serve both constituencies well.

By May of 1920, they were ready to formally launch and signed a

---

[1]Over the course of its nearly one-hundred-year history the Durkee-Mower Company recorded its name both with and without a hyphen. For the reader's ease and consistency this book gives the name a hyphen.

lease for three thousand square feet of production space at 215-217 Burrill Street in Swampscott. As a nod to their days in France, Allen and Fred initially called their product "Toot Sweet Marshmallow Fluff" but quickly (and smartly) dropped that name. The local newspaper recorded their auspicious debut:

New Firm in Town

Two overseas young men, both of the 26th division, Harold A. Durkee and Fred L. Mower, both of this town have formed a partnership in the manufacture of "Marshmallow Fluff," for the wholesale trade. They have secured the rooms formerly occupied by the old Improvement club, renovated them and have installed machinery for the work and are now busily supplying the trade, Mr. Durkee being the selling agent and Mr. Mower attending to the manufacturing end. Both are graduates of the Swampscott High School, both fought in France and are now out to fight their way into the business world, and their friends are convinced they will succeed.

As it turned out, Fred left the Walter M. Lowney Company not long before everything changed there. Walter Lowney was in Atlantic City in the spring of 1921. He had been feeling unwell and his wife, Nettie, hoped some time away from work and the seashore air would do him good. They had just returned from a promenade on the boardwalk and were back in their hotel readying themselves for dinner when Lowney felt a great, sudden pain around his heart and collapsed. He was gone before the doctor arrived. Walter Lowney was sixty-five years old. The entire town of Mansfield mourned his passing, and the day of his funeral, all the town's government offices, factories, and other businesses closed in his honor.

After Lowney's death, his company continued to operate under the leadership of his widow. After a time, the company's rights to individual products and manufacturing facilities were sold. The Boston factories closed. The property on Commercial Street, where Archibald and Fred had met and worked together, is used today as a headquarters for the coast guard.

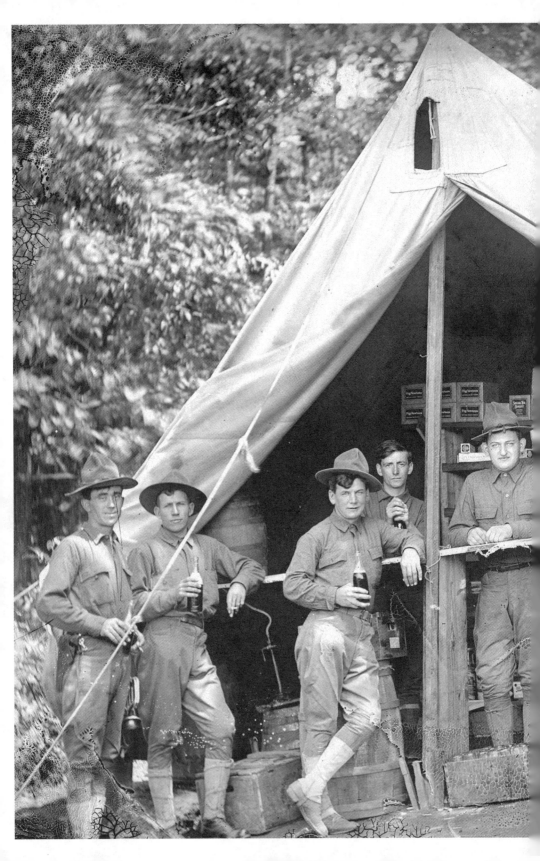

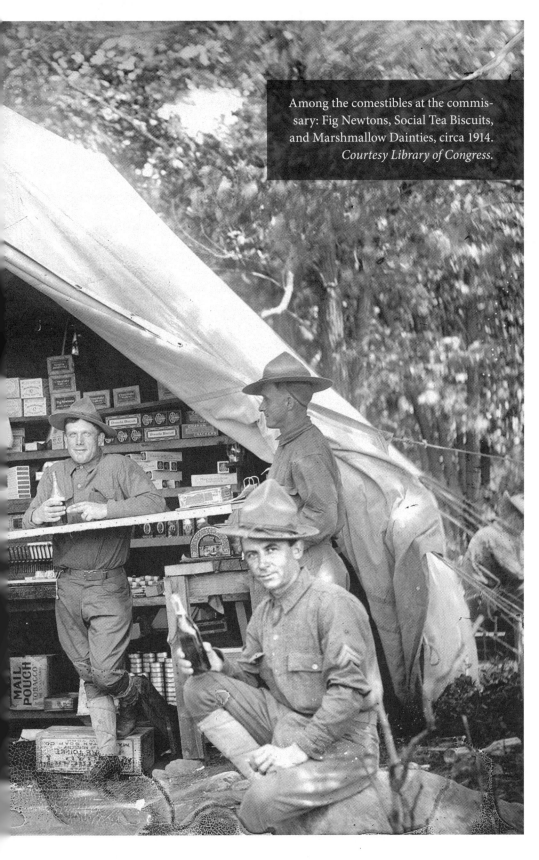

Among the comestibles at the commissary: Fig Newtons, Social Tea Biscuits, and Marshmallow Dainties, circa 1914. *Courtesy Library of Congress.*

fluff

The Canadian branch of the Walter M. Lowney Company, now owned by a subsidiary of Hershey, continues to this day. It manufactures under the Lowney name, and the logo incorporates the same L the company used in its earliest days.

Corporate ownership changed several times, but the Mansfield plant continued to manufacture chocolate through the end of the twentieth century. Eighty-three employees were still coming to work at the factory Lowney built when, in 2009, the machines fell silent. The owner, Archer Daniels Midland Company, one of the world's largest cocoa and chocolate manufacturers, moved what remained of its Mansfield operation to Pennsylvania. The old Lowney property was sold to residential developers who are converting it into loft apartments appropriately dubbed "The Chocolate Factory." Their marketing slogan? "Home, Sweet Home."

Archibald continued in confections for a number of years. As he grew older, the manual work of the factory grew more challenging. During the Great Depression, Archibald was in his sixties and out of work. As part of a government program in 1939, he served as a bookkeeping assistant but the work wasn't steady and he was employed for just thirteen weeks. But retirement was near and his sons were thriving now with lives of their own: John, after studying cello at Boston University, performed with the Boston Pops. With a Ph.D. in music, he was a teacher, living with his family on Long Island. Leo was a teacher as well, teaching high school and living with his wife and son in a small town in New York.

After retiring, Archibald and Elizabeth lived for a number of years on the second floor of a two-family house on Somerville's Summer Street, just outside of Union Square. Archibald's hair had gone pure white but remained a tousled tangle. Lizzy was still technically a redhead, though the color was a particularly sharp orange from a bottle.

Time passed and Leo died at fifty-five, leaving just John to worry about his aging parents, who were both becoming forgetful. One day, when out walking their dog, Archibald became so disoriented that he was unable to find his way home. Even though the couple had little in savings, they were able to move together into St. Patrick's Manor in Boston, a nursing home run by the Catholic Church. Archie and Lizzy had been married sixty-two years when she passed away in the autumn of 1963. Archibald passed away just eight months later. He was ninety-one.

Their grandson, John Jr., recounts warm visits with Archibald and Lizzy in the 1940s, a big white tin filled with handmade hard candies always on the kitchen table. After selling the recipe and showing Fred and Allen how to make Marshmallow Fluff, Archibald Query and the men of Durkee-Mower didn't stay in touch, but Archibald's favorite sandwich remained peanut butter and bananas with Fluff.

Courtesy Durkee-Mower.

Getting to Know
Marshmallow Cream

HAVE you ever truly considered the marshmallow? What exactly is in there? Sugar, of course, but what else? And what makes Fluff (or marshmallow cream to be exact) so sticky and… fluffy? As it turns out, we need to go back a couple of centuries and travel halfway across the globe to really appreciate the utter charm of this fascinating foodstuff. In fact, we have to go to the root—the root of the marshmallow plant, that is, a perennial native to North Africa, Western Asia, and Europe.

Marshmallow
The ancient Egyptians were the first to turn the sap of the marshmallow root into a candy, mixing it with nuts and honey to form a sweet cake reserved for nobles and the gods. The ancient Greek and Indian cultures embraced its healing properties, and through the centuries, marshmallow has remained a popular herbal remedy. Like okra and slippery elm, marshmallow is a mucilaginous food, gooey and viscous. That coating quality cools and supports the body's own mucosa (like the membranes of the digestive and respiratory systems). It is believed that eating the sap of the marshmallow root or drinking a tea made from its dried herb soothes digestion, quiets coughs, and comforts sore throats.

Parisian pharmacists, seeking to make the medicinal sap more palatable, whipped it with sugar, which was similarly thought to hold restorative powers. In the 1800s, however, French confectioners gave up the medicinal pretext and replaced mallow sap with gelatin to bind aerated egg whites and sugar into delicious chewy pillows: marshmallows. While the mallow root was no longer used, the confection's name held fast. By the early 1900s, marshmallows were widely available—using those novel starch mogul machines—in a wide variety of molded shapes: fish, cones, rabbits, and oddly enough, very popular bananas. These fashionable treats were often toasted or dipped in chocolate and coconut. In fancier presentations, they were sandwiched between cookies. Marshmallow-roasting parties became the rage in the 1920s. Trendsetters gathered in circles, each holding a stick with a marshmallow on the end—sort of the flapper version of the 1970s fondue pot.

Cooks were soon incorporating marshmallow into their dishes, both the formed version as well as a softer, looser cream. The latter concoction was initially called "marshmallow paste," but was more appetizingly renamed "crème." Eventually, it became "marshmallow cream." Modern-day marshmallow creams are not made with marshmallow sap *or* gelatin. Though today's cynical consumers might assume they contain unpronounceable chemicals, they are generally composed of four basic ingredients: sugar, vanilla, egg whites, and corn syrup.

Sugar

Sugar has ancient roots in India. It appears in Sanskrit texts written between 1500 and 500 BCE and is referenced in the Hebrew Bible's books of Isaiah and Jeremiah, both written before 600 BCE. The Egyptians, however, were the first to convert cane juice into crystallized sugar, using clarification and condensation methods that remain, in principle, unchanged today. You can even see the Arab root for the word sugarcane—*qandi*—in the English word "candy."

When sugar first came to Europe is a mystery. It may have come to Spain in 650 CE during the Arab conquests, or soldiers returning from the Crusades in 1099 CE might have brought it. However, it was the Venetians—who learned about the Egyptian refining process from Marco Polo—who ultimately dominated the European sugar market. The Venetians essentially had a monopoly on the sugar trade throughout the fifteenth century, importing cane and processing it in their own

Revere Sugar Refinery, 1876. *Courtesy Boston Public Library.*

refineries. Eventually the rest of the continent caught on, establishing their own sources of sugarcane and developing refineries.

Columbus brought the sugarcane crop to the East Indies in 1493. By 1509, sugar was produced in Haiti and the Dominican Republic. Portugal sourced cane from Madeira in the Canary Islands, and then eastern Africa and Brazil. Sugar reached England a little later, arriving hand-in-hand with imported tea and coffee. The English established their first refinery with cane sourced from their territories in Barbados and Jamaica. In the American colonies, domestic honey and maple were readily available sweeteners but, following the tastes of Britain, sugar was preferred.

Even before the candy revolution of the twentieth century, sugar was big business. In the eighteenth century, sugar alone made up one-third of Europe's entire economy. In the American colonies, Britain's effort to limit imports of sugar was a key grievance spurring calls for independence. This isn't to imply that sugar was consumed like it is today. While European royalty enjoyed the luxury of sugary foods, until the mid-nineteenth century, people used sugar primarily for medicinal purposes. They believed sugar could cure almost every ailment, from ulcers to headaches to the pain of childbirth.

Refined sugar, the kind in your sugar bowl, is pure sucrose, a natural carbohydrate present in all green plants. Two plants that contain high levels of sucrose are sugarcane, a tropical grass containing 12 to 14 percent sucrose, and sugar beets, a root vegetable that grows in temperate climates and contains 16 to 18 percent sucrose. In the United States, the majority of refined sugar is sourced from sugarcane.

The need for sugar has had far-reaching and devastating implications. The cultivation and processing of sugarcane, especially in the days before industrialization, was miserable, labor-intensive work. The plantations of the New World were unable to source enough workers among indigenous people and turned to slaves kidnapped from Africa.[1] Over the next four centuries, Europeans and Americans enslaved Africans to plant, harvest, and process sugarcane. This legacy has impacted every aspect of global and American history, instituting patterns of racism and economic inequality that continue into the present day.

American farmers began growing sugarcane in the eighteenth century, and by the mid-nineteenth century, landowners established plantations in Louisiana, Alabama, Mississippi, the Carolinas, Tennessee, Texas, Georgia, and Florida. Despite this growth, domestic yields met only a third of the demand, and American cane contained less sugar than crops in the West Indies, where conditions are better for cultivation. By the late 1800s, American sugar refineries were sourcing their cane primarily from Cuba and Hawaii.

Sugarcane processing consists of two steps: transforming the cane into raw sugar (done near the cane fields) and refining the sugar (done in the market area where the sugar is sold and consumed). Immediately after workers harvest the plants, they clean and shred the sugarcane. They then add hot water to dissolve and extract the sugars as rollers squeeze the cane juice from the pulp. The dark green cane juice is then clarified using milk of lime and carbon dioxide, creating a chemical reaction that helps eliminate the non-sugar plant material. In a series

---

[1] Incidentally, the Durkee family can trace their ancestry to the sugar fields of the Caribbean through William Durkee (Durgy). Durkee was enslaved (likely by Oliver Cromwell) in Ireland and sent to work the sugar plantations of Barbados in the mid-1600s. In 1663, he arrived in Massachusetts Bay Colony as an indentured servant to the merchant Thomas Bishop, becoming the first Irishman to settle here. Almost all Durkees in the United States and Canada are descended from one of his three sons.

of kettles, the filtered juice is then boiled in multiple stages to reduce the water content. In the last kettle, workers put pulverized sugar into the syrup to facilitate the creation of a thick mass of sugar crystals. A centrifuge then spins the crystals dry, yielding richly colored, heavy chunks of raw sugar ready for transport.

In the second stage—refining—raw sugar is processed into consumer goods, such as granulated white sugar, molasses, and other food products. Just as in the earlier field-side stage, water is first added to the raw sugar, loosening the molasses and creating what refiners call "magma." Centrifuges spin the magma to separate the sugar crystals from the molasses. The crystals are then washed, dissolved in lye and carbon dioxide, and filtered of impurities until a clear, concentrated sugar syrup forms. Water is evaporated from the syrup in kettles once again, and the liquid is seeded with fine crystals to encourage their formation. Finally, the sugar crystals are washed, spun yet again, and tumble-dried to remove any remaining moisture. The result is white refined sugar, ready to use.

As early as the late 1700s, shrewd sugar manufacturers recognized the labor-intensive processing of this commodity could benefit from mechanization. The first steam-powered sugar mill began operations in Jamaica in 1768. In the mid-1800s, to increase fuel efficiency and reduce waste, refiners developed a closed kettle system using vacuum pans. They further improved fuel efficiency by putting the vacuum pans in sequence, each held at a lower pressure than the previous one.

The first sugar refinery in the American colonies opened in 1689 in New York City. Bostonians weren't far behind; Ezechiel Cheever operated a refinery in Charlestown from 1721 to 1766. By 1810, there were thirty-three sugar refineries in the United States.

Innovation in sugar manufacturing continued. Until the late nineteenth century, refined sugar was molded into solid blocks, loaves, or cones. Consumers used a sugar nipper or auger to break off the quantity they needed and then grated or ground the pieces into the desired consistency.

The Boston Sugar Refinery in East Boston first developed granulated sugar in 1853. Instead of molding the moist refined sugar, the East Boston factory worked it with wooden rakes over a big steam table, roughly twenty feet long and five feet wide. This process dried and separated the crystals, which were then captured and sorted using various mesh sieves. Later, refiners mechanized the process by churning the drying sugar in large, steam-heated, revolving wood or iron cylinders. A series of buckets lifted the sugar then passed it through mesh screens that sorted the grades for packaging. Sugar companies found it was easier to package granulated sugar into precisely weighed parcels ready for commercial and home applications.

Refining at such a high level also made the sugar less susceptible to adulteration, a common practice in the days before strong food regulations. Before industrial advances dramatically increased production, sugar was expensive, kept in locked boxes with the keys held closely by the lady of the house or the apothecary. The best quality, most highly refined sugar was a twinkling, bright white. Unscrupulous sellers seeking top dollar would often artificially lighten the color, adding gypsum or plaster of Paris and a bluing agent to provide a bright sparkle. To increase the volume, sand was a cheap extender.

Sugar wasn't the only product assailed. Through the 1800s, as life became increasingly urban and personal relationships between food manufacturers, peddlers, and consumers weakened, food contamination became far more commonplace. Life expectancies dropped for city dwellers, a phenomenon directly attributed to corrupted food. Maleficent suppliers and merchants colored watered-down milk with chalk, mixed gravel into black pepper, and put sulfuric acid in vinegars. Under the direction of Harvey Washington Wiley, a series of national studies in the 1880s found nearly every food product on the market was adulterated or mislabeled. Confections were far from immune: chocolate contained lead, brick dust was found in nougat, shellac was used for candy shells, and the list goes on. State regulations offered little protection and enforcement was weak. Poisonous preservatives, dangerous dyes, and unsanitary meat processing plants culminated in a major public health crisis at the end of the nineteenth century.

In Massachusetts, Ellen Swallow Richards helped set the stage for national reform. In 1870, she enrolled as the first woman at the Massachusetts Institute of Technology (MIT) where she studied chemistry. An environmental chemist, she conducted important studies on water, food, and air quality. Richards' study on Massachusetts drinking water established water-quality standards across America and led to Boston's construction of the first modern sewage treatment system. Her 1885 study of staple groceries, commissioned by the Massachusetts Board of Health and titled *Food Materials and Their Adulterations,* highlighted issues of food safety and led to state regulation on the issue. Richards' focus on public health, the science of the home, and her support of women's education made her a leader in the burgeoning field of home economics.

American women, tasked with purchasing and preparing food for their families, were increasingly concerned about food safety. Armed with a growing number of studies and allied through women's clubs, consumer groups, and political action committees, they fought for stronger food safety laws. Through their advocacy, the federal government passed the Pure Food and Drug Act in 1906. A truth-in-labeling law, it defined misbranding and adulteration, established penalties, and addressed inconsistencies in states' rules. In 1938, gaps in the Pure Food and Drug Act were addressed by the federal Food, Drug, and Cosmetic Act (FDCA), which expanded the scope of federal regulation, better defined adulteration, required ingredients of nonstandard foods to be listed on labels, and set mandatory sanitation standards for food preparation. The FDCA remains the primary legislation regulating American foods today.

The price fluctuations and sourcing of sugar were major challenges for confectioners in the first part of the twentieth century. The market volatility reflected power dynamics within the industry. Similar to John D. Rockefeller who dominated oil commodities, Henry Osborne Havemeyer, owner of New York's largest sugar refinery, was America's "sugar king." As one of the nation's robber barons, his so-called Sugar Trust controlled production and set prices across the country. Under Havemeyer, the twenty-three operational refineries in 1887 dwindled to just five. By 1907, the Sugar Trust owned or controlled 98 percent of the sugar-processing industry in the entire United States. Despite court efforts to break up the monopoly, the business practices and dominance of the Sugar Trust remained in place well into the twentieth century. Today, the company Havemeyer built, American Sugar Refining, continues to prevail, selling under the Domino brand.

March 1888
of H2SO4
equations:
III Test for a sulphide,
IV Define the terms acid
and illustrate by

Ellen Swallow Richards (top row, far left) and her class at the Women's Laboratory at the Massachusetts Institute of Technology, 1888. *Courtesy MIT Museum.*

fluff

Vanilla

Many people think vanilla is boring, an anonymous background player. Those with more attentive palates, however, appreciate the exotic fruit in all its fragrant complexity. For products like marshmallow cream, vanilla is the quiet workhorse that subtly enhances whatever it touches.

Vanilla was treasured for centuries as medicine, perfume, and flavoring by the indigenous American peoples where the tropical orchid is native. The Spanish brought vanilla pods to Europe, where they were embraced for their fragrance and flavor. Until the mid-nineteenth century, Mexico was the primary commercial producer of vanilla.

Vanilla is a notoriously challenging crop. The plants flourish only in smaller-scaled plots, limiting the creation of large, centralized plantations. Blooms open just one day a year, during which farmers must pollinate each by hand. Then they must pluck, cure, dry, condition, and sort the mature fruit before it is ready for market. From beginning to end, this takes close to twelve months. Vanilla became more accessible in the 1870s when producers acquired a better understanding of the plant and more efficient processing methods—just in time for the world's love affair with confections.

Larger and higher quality yields weren't enough to staunch the demand, though. Confectioners, bakers, and perfumers, looking to meet consumer expectations at a lower cost, sought cheaper approximations of vanilla's flavor and aroma. In 1858, chemists isolated vanillin, the primary component of pure vanilla extract. This discovery led to the commercial production of semi-synthetic vanillin by the end of the century. Using plentiful and accessible compounds sourced from clove oil and then wood pulp, manufacturers were able to produce large quantities of vanillin cheaply. Soon, even the most modest mass-produced foods of the early twentieth century were able to mimic the exotic flavor of vanilla.

Egg Whites

Egg whites are the albumen of chicken eggs, clear and thick with a mucus-like viscosity, reminiscent of marshmallow sap. Commercial manufacturers use dried egg whites because eliminating moisture makes the whites less perishable and removes the need for refrigeration, resulting in a lower risk of contamination. Also, because egg whites are 90 percent water, the condensed, dried form is significantly cheaper to ship and store. Dried eggs have been widely available since the early 1900s.

Commercial dried egg whites are produced in two ways. Spray-dried egg whites are the most common, made by shooting atomized liquid egg whites into a stream of hot air, instantly producing a fine powder. Alternatively, the pan-dried form is produced the way it sounds. Manufacturers spread the egg whites onto pans to speed evaporation and then break down the resulting protein into either flake, granular, or powdered form. Modern manufacturers sometimes remove the naturally occurring glucose of the egg white before drying to improve shelf life. They also produce a specialized product called "high-whip dried egg white" by adding a tiny amount of sodium lauryl sulfate before drying to achieve a fluffier egg foam. Spray-dried egg whites have a tendency to clump when reconstituted, so marshmallow cream makers generally prefer the pan-dried type.

Corn Syrup

Corn syrup, a clear, colorless, thick liquid, was first developed in 1812 by the Russian chemist Gottlieb Kirchhoff by heating a mixture of cornstarch under pressure with a catalyst of dilute hydrochloric acid. In the United States, readily available sugarcane made the need for alternative sweeteners less urgent, and therefore was relatively slow to develop the technology. Karo, the brand now synonymous with corn syrup, was founded in 1902 and continues to thrive today.

Corn syrup adds some sweetness and flavor to marshmallow cream, but its primary function is to support and contribute to the volume created by the whipped egg whites. Likewise, its addition creates a glossy appearance and maintains a smooth texture, free of crystallized sugar.

While corn syrup makers could interrupt the hydrolysis process at key points to create different flavor and color grades, nearly all corn syrup on the market today uses the same base syrup and adds flavoring. In the case of Karo, adding vanilla flavor and salt makes light corn syrup; dark corn syrup uses molasses, caramel color and flavor, and salt.

fluff

The corn syrup used in Marshmallow Fluff, and commonly used in homemade candies, jellies, and jams, shouldn't be confused with high-fructose corn syrup (HFCS). "Regular" corn syrup is glucose sugar while HFCS is further refined into fructose, a sugar more than twice as sweet. Too much of any sugar is a health concern, but HFCS has caused worries because of its possible link to heart disease, cancer, and liver failure. From a health standpoint, the difference between the two types is significant.

Making Marshmallow Cream

In composition and technique, marshmallow cream is actually more like a meringue than a formed marshmallow. Like meringues, marshmallow cream requires only egg whites and sugar; it doesn't need gelatin or another firming agent to hold its shape.

Meringues predate marshmallow confections. The first recipes for meringues date to the sixteenth century and combined frothed egg whites with sugar and cream of tartar. As confectioners entered the Industrial Era, they continued to make meringues with the same well-established techniques and familiar ingredients, albeit a bit more quickly.

Frothing egg whites to create a meringue seems simple enough, but consider the effort it takes to incorporate enough air into beaten egg whites so that the resulting bubbles hold their shape. There's documentation dating back to the sixteenth century of cooks using bundles of cleaned twigs to whisk egg whites with cream of tartar to create foamy meringue mixtures. As you might expect, twigs or other early tools like fingers, spoons, and blades weren't the most effective. Recipes from the eighteenth and early nineteenth centuries detail cake batters requiring beating times of three hours. (Encouragingly, these recipes offered hints for how to cope with the inevitable fatigue.)

Help arrived, at last, in the 1850s. Tinsmiths fashioned a variety of flat and balloon-shaped wire whisks and then found new and ingenious means to make them twirl and agitate. There was such a stampede of new products and patented ideas that one newspaper said of the early Hale Aerating Egg-beater, "The present is truly the age of invention."

Within the decade, manufacturers seemingly achieved perfection with a hand-cranked eggbeater that would become a household standard for the ages. It's shocking today to put the invention into context. Technology had moved forward in so many areas and grown more scientifically complex. The steam train, the telegraph, color photography, even the machine gun—all of these innovations predated the invention of the eggbeater. This modest invention transformed work in the kitchen for generations of women.

The Dover Stamping and Manufacturing Company in Cambridge, Massachusetts made its model by conjoining two balloon beaters with double-sided, cast iron gears. When the handle is spun, the interlocking whisks revolve in opposite directions. Members of the culinary world, their arms limp with weariness, were positively ecstatic at this revolutionary improvement. In 1875, one cookbook writer in Chicago went so far as to declare, "As long as there are eggs to beat, give me Dover or give me death!"

Now that liquids could be efficiently whipped, those grueling recipes calling for volumes of frothed egg whites were suddenly all the rage. While it continued to make and sell a whole catalog of wares, the Dover company focused on its famous eggbeaters. In the early twentieth century, 250 workers labored in the Cambridge factory, churning out the familiar kitchen tool. Their model was so well known that for decades the generic name for an eggbeater was simply a "Dover."

Power mixers weren't far behind. Rufus Eastman invented the first one in Boston in 1885. His patent details motorized beaters that, when placed "in a suitable vessel," can mix creams, eggs, and liquors. Electric mixers were widely available thereafter, including a notable series of standing mixers created in 1908 by the Hobart Manufacturing Company in Ohio. But it

Do you know that the genuine & original Dover EGG BEATER is Manufactured in Cambridge by The Dover Stamping & Manufacturing Co. ?

The invention of the Dover eggbeater revolutionized American kitchens. *Courtesy Cambridge Public Library.*

wasn't until after World War I that household models became common-place. The Sunbeam Mixmaster by the Chicago Flexible Shaft Company and Hobart's KitchenAid Food Preparer were leading models.

There's no way that super-sticky, super-smooth, super-thick Marshmallow Fluff could be whipped up by anything less than a power-mixing machine equipped with a whisk that maximizes the development of air bubbles. Access to this equipment would have been essential for Archibald Query to develop his recipe and manufacture Marshmallow Fluff. And decades later, pinpointing this magic moment became a matter of life and death for Durkee-Mower.

Anyone who's tried to rescue a falling meringue will tell you that fat is the enemy of perfectly peaked egg whites. Fat breaks down the albumen, limiting the ability of egg whites to hold their shape. While all meringue recipes require the meticulous separation of the fat-bearing yolks, some go so far as to instruct the cook to wipe bowls, beaters, and other utensils with white vinegar to eliminate any trace of fat that might remain from previous use. It's here that the distinction of marshmallow cream from formed marshmallows is most apparent. Many people wonder why there is no chocolate version of Marshmallow Fluff. This is because the fats within cocoa butter would make the delicate froth fall flat. While you can easily find a chocolate marshmallow, marshmallow cream lacks a firming agent sturdy enough to combat the fat. To enjoy this amazing flavor combination at home, however, simply add a heaping spoon of cream to the top of a cup of hot cocoa!

✦

So how exactly is Marshmallow Fluff made? The recipe Allen and Fred acquired from Archibald Query has essentially remained the same since 1917. But what's the alchemy in this four-ingredient concoction? Homemade marshmallow cream becomes flat within a day, so how does Marshmallow Fluff stay so light and fluffy for months?

Durkee-Mower isn't telling. The company has cultivated a Willy

Wonka-like air of detachment. Access to the factory is rare and the company is notoriously private, a frustration to Fluff fans. But this reticence is understandable. The makers of Fluff, like every other confectioner, have no way to protect their primary corporate asset from copycats. Most businesses can use a patent to halt others from replicating their product, but marshmallow cream is ineligible. To qualify for patent, an invention must be considered novel and nonobvious. While it is a tricky task to achieve just the right consistency, the process of whipping egg whites with sugar has been around for centuries. As far as the United States patent office is concerned, there's no invention in Marshmallow Fluff or, indeed, any comparable recipe. This makes Durkee-Mower exceedingly vulnerable. Marshmallow Fluff is the only product it sells, and its most essential asset—the recipe—could be stolen and replicated at any moment without consequence.

All confectioners who combine common ingredients using well-known techniques face the same challenge. M&Ms are candy-coated chocolate pieces; a Sugar Daddy is a rectangle of caramel on a stick; Almond Joy is coconut topped with almonds and covered in chocolate. It might be tricky, but an experienced candy maker can replicate almost every candy concoction out there.

Confectioners can and do use trademark protection to avoid the unlicensed use of their established brands, but a recognizable name and a familiar package only go so far in a fickle marketplace. One famous story of recipe theft emerged from the epic battle between the world's candy kings, Mars and Hershey. In the 1950s, the Mars Company in Britain produced a chocolate bar called Bounty—a duplicate of Hershey's chocolate-covered coconut bar called Mounds. The facsimile became such a bestseller that today most consumers in the United Kingdom and Canada are unaware of the original candy bar. Hershey's, the company that first developed the concept, sees none of those profits.

It's no surprise then that confectioners rely on secrecy to protect their assets. There are numerous industry stories of gauges calibrated to read inaccurate temperatures, of visitors to candy factories blindfolded with all the drama of a spy movie, of espionage, misdirection, and stony silence. Mars is particularly notorious; when Forrest Mars, Sr. died, the loss went unacknowledged to maintain privacy. The culture at Durkee-Mower isn't that extreme, but Don and Jon Durkee, the two generations who run the company today, hold their company's information tightly.[2]

✦

A confluence of forces in Boston had enabled the birth of Marshmallow Fluff. The only thing missing was an audience with an appetite for this sticky, sweet spread. One highly influential Bostonian with a panache for cooking and a hankering for sweets was there to assist.

In 1896, Boston's Fannie Farmer, one of the nation's most highly regarded cookbook authors and culinary instructors, first referenced "marshmallow paste" in her groundbreaking tome, the *Boston Cooking-School Cook Book*. In the chapter of cake fillings and frostings, Fannie included a recipe that called for melting marshmallows with a little hot water over a double boiler, then gradually beating in a boiling syrup of sugar and milk. When the mixture is cool enough to spread, a bit of vanilla is added.

Fannie was foremost an educator, and her scientific approach to measuring ingredients and cooking technique made her one of the most esteemed cooking teachers at the turn of the twentieth century and a leader in the home economics movement. Before her work in the late 1800s, there was no consistency in recipes. While she didn't define them, Fannie popularized the common measurements of cups, tablespoons, and teaspoons in American cooking. She emphasized the importance of diligently using measured level ingredients to maintain uniform results, giving her the moniker of the "Mother of Level Measurements."

In 1902, she established Miss Farmer's School of Cookery on Huntington Avenue in Boston and offered programs for home cooks as well as professionals. The school's folksy name belied its rigor. Along

---

[2]While I was given open access to the half dozen scrapbooks where the company's history is gathered, Durkee-Mower wasn't actively involved in the research of this book. Over ten years of casual conversations with the Durkee-Mower staff provided me with a wealth of knowledge, but neither Don Durkee, nor his son Jon, would agree to a formal interview. Don claimed he was too busy, while Jon said he was too shy.

with demonstrations and hands-on classes in "advanced cookery," the school's summer program included extensive training in nutrition and applied organic chemistry, with specific workshops for professionals working in food management in hospitals, schools, and other institutions. She had a particular interest in nutrition, addressing the dietary needs of children, convalescents, and those with diabetes. She was a leader in her field. Even though Harvard University did not admit women at the time, Farmer was hired as a lecturer at its prestigious medical school.

For generations of Americans, a Fannie Farmer cookbook was their first and only cookbook. Dog-eared, stained copies were (and still are) lovingly passed on as family heirlooms. Farmer wrote numerous cookbooks, including evocative titles such as *Chafing Dish Possibilities, What to Have for Dinner, A Book of Good Dinners for My Friend*, and her 1912 volume, *A New Book of Cookery: Eight-hundred and Sixty Recipes Covering the Whole Range of Cookery*. It was the publication of her *Boston Cooking-School Cook Book,* however, that firmly established Fannie Farmer as the quintessential culinary authority in New England. She's best known for this book, which is now in its thirteenth edition.

As Laura Shapiro writes in *The Oxford Companion to Sugar and Sweets,* "Farmer never met a marshmallow she did not like and could not mix into ice cream, frosting, or especially gelatin. Her salads were often as sweet as desserts." In *A New Book of Cookery,* the sequel to her opus written on behalf of the Boston School of Cookery, Farmer shares recipes for Marshmallow Hot Chocolate, Marshmallow Gingerbread, Marshmallow Ice Cream, Marshmallow Mint Bonbons, a marshmallow sauce, and something called Marshmallow Tea—basically crackers with melted marshmallows and a cherry on top. Illustrative of her sweet tooth, a full third of the book—126 pages—is devoted to cakes and frostings, dessert puddings, cookies, and candy. Farmer's recipes installed marshmallow cream in kitchens across New England, and her influence on national tastes can't be overestimated. For decades, she spread her marshmallow enthusiasm to thousands of students and they eagerly followed her lead. Many of them found employment creating recipes for local confectioners who commissioned cookbooks under the company name. Maria Willet Howard, one of

Farmer's students, wrote the Walter M. Lowney Company cookbook, published in 1907. Howard's cookbook includes one of the earliest recipes for chocolate brownies. Acolytes throughout the twentieth century were creating recipes that would regularly appear in New England newspapers, in countless cookbooks, and on the radio, recommending marshmallows and marshmallow cream as an easy way to add sweetness and volume to both sweet and savory dishes.

Courtesy Durkee-Mower.

✦

To meet the demand of consumers hungry for marshmallow cream, commercial producers sprung up across the country. In 1913 Philadelphia, Whitman's—best known today for the ubiquitous drugstore chocolates, the Whitman Sampler—produced Marshmallow Whip. Hippolyte Marshmallow Creme reigned in the South. Strong brands emerged in the Midwest as well. For the most part, they are all long forgotten. Among the relics in the Durkee-Mower archive is a can of Three Millers Marshmallow Cream of Boston, likely from the 1910s. There's also a poster for May's Marshmallow Cream, which promises to be "Sweet and Palatable as Cow's Cream" with "None of the Fishy Taste and Odor of other Emulsions."

But before Durkee-Mower, Whitman's, Hippolyte, and even before Archibald Query's marshmallow cream, there was already a well-established company beating egg whites and sugar just outside Boston in Melrose, Massachusetts: Emma Curtis' Snowflake Marshmallow Crème.

Under the name Emma E. Curtis Company, siblings Emma Curtis and Amory Revere Curtis manufactured several products, including Orangeade Paste, a concentrated orange syrup to mix with water for a refreshing drink; Mai-po-lex, a "compound Vegetable Flavor tasting like maple, but containing no maple sap, syrup, or sugar"; and later, Melrose Marshmallows. It was Emma Curtis' Snowflake Marshmallow Crème, however, that would emerge as their signature product.

Amory Curtis had a talent for chemistry. A graduate of Boston English High School, he was offered a place at MIT, but financial constraints forced him to decline and enter the business world. In the mid-1890s, with his partner Jack Moore, Amory and his company manufactured fruit extracts and syrups and sold hardware for soda fountains. Meanwhile, Emma, unmarried and fifteen years his senior, was working as a bookkeeper and becoming a businesswoman in her own right.[3]

In 1901, Amory purchased the row of lots making up the entire east

---

[3]In 1900, the Curtis family—Amory, Emma, and their aging parents—were living together in Somerville at 23 Mount Vernon Street, ironically less than two miles away from Archibald Query, that young candy man just starting out in the big city.

Emma and Amory on Crystal Street in Melrose, circa 1910. *Courtesy of Melrose Public Library.*

The interior of the Emma E. Curtis Company's factory, circa 1910. *Courtesy of Melrose Public Library.*

side of Crystal Street in Melrose, a suburb just seven miles north of Boston. Melrose incorporated as a city just the year before, and it was growing fast; the population doubled between 1890 and 1910. Crystal Street was a quiet side road overlooking Ell Pond and just a ten-minute walk from the city's business center, making it a great location to live and work. Amory and his new wife, Mabel Greene, a dressmaker from Melrose, took up residence at 17 Crystal Street. Emma soon followed, taking up residence at 33 Crystal Street, adjacent to their new factory.

In December 1913, the siblings sought additional staff for their growing business. An advertisement in the *Melrose Free Press* called for women aged sixteen and over to join them. The gender divide in their factory was comparable to those of other confectionery companies; men brought in the raw materials, oversaw the hot kettles, and managed transport of the finished product, while women were charged with packaging, marketing, and direct sales. In a job posting composed by Emma, she wrote: "I desire only refined, intelligent young women of the best school, church, or employer references."

Amory, a tall man with a very slender build despite a lifetime of sampling sweets, identified foremost as a scientist. He worked behind the scenes, developing the production processes and creating the equipment used to manufacture both the confections and the packaging. Amory oversaw the calibration of the factory's gauges—and like other paranoid confectioners, he turned a dial to mislead anyone who might try to steal their recipes.

Emma was the public face of the company, overseeing the finances, marketing, and sales. Because marshmallow cream was a relatively new product, Emma developed recipes and published tiny recipe books, measuring about two square inches, which were used to promote its Snowflake Marshmallow Crème. Simpler recipes included various sandwich combinations, as well as basic sauces that consisted of water, milk, or coffee mixed with the marshmallow.

Emma supplied the first documented pairing of marshmallow cream and peanut butter in 1914 with a brief mention in one of her recipe books. In the 1916 edition, she wrote: "Use any crisp unsweetened cracker spread with Snowflake Marshmallow Crème and place one on top of the other. This is an attractive and dainty sandwich for afternoon teas or the picnic basket, and may be varied as fancy dictates, by adding chopped nuts, olives, and peanut butter with the Marshmallow or by using thin slices of bread and butter or cake instead of the crackers."

Two years later, she had developed what would be dubbed the Fluffernutter by Durkee-Mower's advertising team in 1958. In 1918, Emma suggested the combination of marshmallow cream and peanut butter between slices of oat bread (thankfully skipping the olives), and she named it "The Liberty Sandwich." The name may have reflected the patriotism of the World War I years, during which Americans were encouraged to forego meat at least one day a week. But it's also possible that Emma was flaunting her pedigree: the siblings were the great-great-great grandchildren of Paul Revere.

A full-figured Emma often appeared in the company's publicity photos, dressed in an apron and white cotton mop hat with her hair swept into a bun. She was featured in the corner of what was likely the factory's test kitchen, carefully measuring ingredients into a beaker. She comes across as part scientist, part colonial grandma—a culinary Marie Curie.

Emma's cotton mop hat was the standard costume of all female employees at the company, both for factory workers and the women offering samples of marshmallow cream on crackers. The hats were reminiscent of colonial America—it's easy to picture Martha Washington wearing one—and the association was deliberate. A wave of nationalism swept the United States in the 1910s and 1920s, and there was great interest in colonial New England. Americans idealized this period, feeling it epitomized the best of the American spirit: morally wholesome, hardworking and tenacious, and independent yet strong with familial and community ties. There was a revival in colonial home decor and design during these years as well. (Throughout the region, colonial houses have endured.) Companies worked to associate themselves with this bygone era to express how their products aligned with these early American values. While the Curtis siblings never overtly mentioned their pedigree as direct descendants of Paul Revere, they subtly evoked patriotism and colonial history as part of a broader national trend.

The company did, however, place Emma's female identity front and

DESSERTS of QUALITY
How to prepare them
by Emma E. Curtis

Courtesy Durkee-Mower.

center in its marketing. The full name of its signature product was Miss Curtis' Snowflake Marshmallow Crème, sometimes called Emma Curtis' Snowflake Marshmallow Crème. Later, when produced under a shortened designation, SMAC, Emma's name as manufacturer was written boldly on labels and promotions, the font size second only to the product name. A 1915 advertisement in the *Pittsburgh Press* put particular emphasis on the point: "Made By A Woman. Used by A Woman." Quality is ensured because it "is a 'homemade' product. Every can of it is put up under the personal direction of Miss Emma Curtis under the most sanitary conditions, at her own home…"

The government was only beginning to regulate food manufacturing and distribution; the Pure Food and Drug Act of 1906 was still new and evolving. Emma's name was a personal guarantee of quality, an assurance that it was wholesomely made by a trusted friend. Women identified with Emma: she was on the label, she was an authority at in-store demonstrations, and she was the author of those helpful recipe books. Who wouldn't have aspired to be like her? Even her home's bucolic setting, "on the shores of beautiful Crystal Lake," inspired visions of tidiness, confidence, and attention to detail.

As Emma and Amory grew older they remained active in the company, but their involvement slowed. In their company's waning days, Amory would still personally whip up the marshmallow cream for the Brigham's Ice Cream parlor in Boston.

By 1945, after a series of family losses, the siblings decided to shutter the factory. A public auction was held to offload the company's assets. The bulletin proclaimed: "Name, Goodwill, Registered Trade Names, Machinery, and Equipment." Farewell to the twenty-five-gallon Badger beaters, the steam jacketed kettles, and the big copper measuring tanks. Goodbye to the chutes and gauges and thermometers, the capping machine, the timing clocks, every piece, down to the hand dollies, typewriters, and office chairs. If anyone purchased the trade names of "SMAC Marshmallow" or "Snowflake Marshmallow Crème" there is no sign that they ever used them. Just three years later, Emma Curtis died at the age of eighty-six.

Today, beyond some archived photographs and labels, we have little by which to remember Snowflake Marshmallow Crème and Emma and

Amory's company. In May of 1962, two youths robbed the apartment above the factory that Emma once occupied and set fire to the property, burning 33 Crystal Street to the ground.

Orange Marshmallow Custard
By Emma Curtis, "Desserts of Quality: How to Prepare Them," 1916

Cut 2 oranges into small pieces and add 3 tablespoons of Snowflake Marshmallow Crème. Make a custard with 1 pint of milk, bring to boiling, then add 3 even teaspoons of corn starch and the yolks of 3 eggs well beaten. Wet the corn starch first with a little cold milk to prevent its lumping. Cook this custard until fairly thick; then cool and pour over the oranges, stirring slightly. Much of the Snowflake Marshmallow Crème will rise, forming a delicious topping.

Allen Durkee (left) and Fred Mower (right) at a company party, circa 1928. *Courtesy Durkee-Mower.*

A Fluffy Start

WITH the help of its publicists, Durkee-Mower practically turned the story of its scrappy beginning into a legend: two young men with "one barrel of sugar (at 28 cents per pound), a few tin cans, two spoons, one second-hand Ford, and no customers, but plenty of prospects."

They liked to talk about their lack of resources, but it's likely that Allen's father, a general contractor and residential developer, invested in the business to get them started. On April 28, 1920, just two days after registering their first sale, Allen and Fred leased the factory on Burrill Street. Order number one was from Huntoon House, a resort inn in North Sutton, New Hampshire, for three pounds of Marshmallow Fluff. Total invoice: three dollars. By the end of their first year they had sold two thousand cans of hand-packed Marshmallow Fluff and showed a total of six people on the payroll.

As the company grew, Durkee-Mower secured Dunn & Sonigan, a brokerage firm, to go after wholesale deals with area grocery stores and emerging chains. As president, Allen signed the contract, while Fred, the company's treasurer, and Bill Dunn sealed the agreement with a handshake and toothy smiles in front of the factory.

Within six years of launching the Durkee-Mower Company, Allen and Fred served as best men at each other's weddings and became fathers. Allen had welcomed the first two of his three sons and Fred celebrated his only child, a daughter. Family life must have added even more intensity to their business ambitions, but Dinty and Joe (along with their Marshmallow Fluff team) were known to have a bit of fun, too. Holidays and special occasions meant clearing a table on the factory floor where friends and colleagues gathered, cracked open beers, lit up cigars, and joked around on instruments, singing together with full-throated gusto. Around Christmas, a scraggly tree decorated with tinsel and baubles usually sat in the corner beside cases of Fluff awaiting shipment.

In 1924, Fred's father-in-law, Charles Jenkins, joined the team. Charles was a machinist, a skillset not immediately associated with the confectionery field, but Allen and Fred knew that they would need to automate if they were going to produce more Fluff. Charles could design, build, and repair the equipment vital to their plans.

It looks like it worked. By 1929, Durkee-Mower was, by any estimation, selling a lot of Fluff. Less than a decade after making its first small batch, it was shipping a million cases of marshmallow cream each year with gross sales of $120,000 (roughly $1.5 million in today's dollars). With strong sales and efficient production systems in place, what Durkee-Mower now required was space. The company was cramped in

Cocoa

RICH'S INSTANT COCOA

It is truly instant. Place 3 level tablespoons of Rich's Instant Cocoa in a teacup. Add ⅔ cup boiling water and the beverage is ready. A little milk or cream may be added if desired. Serve with a topping of Marshmallow Fluff.

RICH'S INSTANT COCOA with ORANGE JUICE
Full of Vitamines

3 tablespoons Rich's Instant Cocoa
3 tablespoons boiling water
½ cup orange juice
Cracked ice

Dissolve Rich's Instant Cocoa with boiling water. Add cracked ice and orange juice.

RICH'S HOT MOCHA

4 tablespoons Rich's Instant Cocoa
1 cup thin cream
3 cups boiling hot coffee

Pour the hot coffee on the Rich's Instant Cocoa. Rich's Instant Cocoa dissolves instantly. Add the cream. Bring to boiling point. Serve. A delicious drink.

Look for the
Buff and Brown Can
Quality Tells

Courtesy Durkee-Mower.

just three thousand square feet in the Swampscott factory and desperately needed to expand.

Hot cocoa was the answer. Fred was familiar with the process for making a powdered cocoa product from his days at the Walter M. Lowney Company, where such a mix was produced. Durkee-Mower made some exploratory forays into manufacturing hot cocoa powder on its own, but—with limited space and lacking the specialized commercial equipment—it made the most sense to acquire a competitor.

Cream of Chocolate, a brand of powdered instant chocolate drink, had been around since 1890. Chester F. Rich of Waltham, Massachusetts had purchased the Lynn-based company a number of years before and was manufacturing the powdered drink under the name of Rich's Instant Cocoa. His sales strategy was different from Durkee-Mower's: Rich sold his cocoa almost exclusively wholesale to women's organizations, which then resold individual packages for church and club fundraisers. Rich's Instant Cocoa wasn't available in stores, and Chester Rich hadn't exploited the benefits of the grocery trade, which made the deal all the more attractive. The prospect would allow Durkee-Mower to expand its offerings, acquire necessary equipment, and assume a trained staff. The deal was particularly sweet because it included much-needed factory space: a roomy ten-thousand-square-foot industrial building along a rail line on Brookline Street in Lynn. Durkee-Mower bought out the company and took on Chester Rich as a vice president.

Durkee-Mower's move from Swampscott to East Lynn tripled the size of its physical plant. With the addition of the Rich company staff, at the close of 1930, the Durkee-Mower team was ten people strong. Little did Allen and Fred know that the new Lynn site, a creaky, old wooden building, would remain the home of their company into the present day.

For the next eight years, the new chocolate drink was saddled with the unwieldy name of "Durkee-Mower's Instant Sweet Milk Cocoa." (Smarter heads eventually prevailed in 1937, when Durkee-Mower renamed the product Sweeco.) The drink mix contained a "special blend" of cocoa, sugar, full cream milk, and flavoring. To create it, workers combined the ingredients and then poured the mixture onto large trays set upon rolling racks. These racks were wheeled into a large electric oven where they remained for fifteen hours to dehydrate the liquid.

fluff

Once cooled, the resulting cakes were ground into a powder that was packed into flip-top cans.

Durkee-Mower sales agents went to work pitching the product to grocery stores. Advertisements heralded the nutritive powers of milk, chocolate, and sugar—claims that sound absurd by today's standards. "It is the only beverage except milk that is allowed on many training tables and athletic clubs, and is especially recommended for invalids and convalescents and children," declared one ad.

Like Emma Curtis, Durkee-Mower produced recipe books that used both Sweeco and Fluff, together or on their own. Through this marketing, a cup of hot Sweeco with a scoop of melting Fluff on top became a favorite New England combination and was a featured recipe. "Hot Chocolate was never so good—Brisk autumn evenings step up the call for hot chocolate as a favorite drink…. and it's better than ever when it's Sweeco Chocolate topped off with a generous spoonful of Marshmallow Fluff…. the light creamy marshmallow that adds new zest to dozens of dishes."

Sweeco was primarily sold in individual tins, but for a time it was paired with a can of Fluff and packaged in a box. In 1933, Durkee-Mower began putting the two products in identical tins with lids that could be popped off with a coin or spoon. It was a departure from how marshmallow

Making Sweeco.
Courtesy Durkee-Mower.

Fred Mower (right) shakes hands with Bill Dunn of Dunn & Sonigan,
the firm that represented Fluff to the trade. Swampscott, circa 1920s.
Courtesy Durkee-Mower.

creams had been previously packaged and Durkee-Mower recognized
this with an ad declaring, "New! Better! Radically Different!"

Established in its new, expanded facilities with nothing to hold
it back, Durkee-Mower was flying high. After ten years in business,
Allen reported a salary of $30,000 a year, equivalent to $425,000 today. Each year, this dynamic duo recognized the anniversary of their
business with a cake cutting at the factory. Milestone years would get
special fanfare, but each anniversary was given its due with a moment
of appreciation for the company they were building.

Success for Durkee-Mower required more than a strong team inside the factory; it required nurturing loyal customers, making sure
they always reached for Marshmallow Fluff on their grocer's shelves.
Marshmallow Fluff entered the marketplace at a time when cultural
shifts were transforming the business of food manufacturing as well
as the entire American landscape. A revolution in food retailing and
marketing was on the horizon; Durkee-Mower made sure it was going
to rise with the tide.

A 1920s domestic science curriculum was a rigorous combination of practice and theory. *Courtesy Library of Congress.*

Ladies Love Fluff

1920 wasn't *just* the year Fred and Allen founded Durkee-Mower; it was also a monumental year for American women. That August, Congress passed the Nineteenth Amendment to the US Constitution, ensuring a woman's right to vote throughout the United States of America. The constitutional change had been a long time coming; it was first introduced in Congress forty-two years before. During those ensuing decades, suffrage was just one arena for political action by women. Female activists fought on the front lines for public education, worker's rights, temperance, public health improvements, support for immigrants, peace, and more, strengthening their voices and gaining skills in collective action. Through those struggles, women were constructing a new identity, one that used traditional female roles to carve out a new place for women in American public life.

During this time period, science seemed to be the singular solution for every problem. Just as men were inventing increasingly more complex machines and building factories, women, constrained to the domestic sphere, were looking to master the systems and science inherent in *their* work. Tasked with food preparation, household management, early childhood education, and home-based nursing, women turned the home into their laboratories, engaging physics, chemistry, and biology. With scientific rigor and visionary passion, they sought to better society.

fluff

With this scientific approach, women brought greater knowledge and improved status to what was known as "women's work." They organized and called the field of study domestic science, creating curriculums that were taught across the country. This educational movement began in the mid-1800s with the training of poor and immigrant women for domestic service jobs. While some saw the field narrowly—merely the preparation of young women for rote household duties—others envisioned an opportunity to advance women's education and pushed for an approach with greater academic merit. Though still centered on cooking, nursing, and childcare, domestic science provided women with a pathway into the public sphere and professional pursuits. For example, social reformer Catharine Beecher (half sister of abolitionist Harriet Beecher Stowe) wrote books and founded schools that elevated home management to a noble calling of national importance and emphasized the need to effectively prepare women in their role as teachers. Moving beyond the kitchen, Fannie Farmer, domestic scientist and renowned booster of marshmallow cream, did more than teach cooking classes. She was one of a growing number of women leaders in the emerging field of food science, advancing the study and practice of sanitation, nutrition, and food chemistry. Even Ellen Swallow Richards' crucial work in sanitation had grown out of an interest in domestic needs.

Through the twentieth century, as mass production expanded and the middle class emerged, domestic science mutated from these broader academic pursuits and practical skills into consumer education and marketing. Women, the primary decision makers regarding household purchases, became the nation's dominant consumers in this period. Consequently, they also became the targets of massive amounts of advertising. Under this pressure, the domestic sphere shifted away from its origins in science, and the idealized home became a trophy case for the growing middle class. But in its initial formation, domestic science set the groundwork for areas of study in public health, social work and child welfare, education, and consumer protection. In its heyday, the field was a force for positive change for women and all of society.

Unlike the watered-down version at the end of the twentieth century, 1920s domestic science curriculum was a rigorous combination of practice and theory. Sewing classes progressed from needlework and ironing to dress patterns and millinery. The hands-on tasks were put into a broader perspective as students learned about the history of fashion, the construction of textiles, and how to estimate the costs of finished items. Practical cookery moved through the basics of cooking methods like boiling, baking, roasting, and stewing to the more advanced tasks of bread baking, butchery, and food preservation. Food safety, hygiene, and nutrition were all covered in detail. By graduation, students were well-versed in the chemistry that informed soap making, the physics of home systems and appliances, physiology for home-based nursing, and everything in between.

Courtesy Durkee-Mower.

Courtesy Boston Public Library.

The nation as a whole began to appreciate women as mothers, wives, and homemakers, publicly recognizing how they were tasked with nurturing America's workers, soldiers, and leaders. In this way, the state of the home had powerful consequences for all of society. Housework became a moral issue and a reflection of the country's Christian values with "cleanliness is next to Godliness" as a commonly accepted trope. Safe and clean homes, intelligent and healthy children, strong and steady husbands—these were national assets and deemed a women's responsibility.

To manage the technological changes in their twentieth-century homes, women knew ongoing education was essential. A better understanding of the nature of disease and health led to a shift away from Victorian draperies and enclosed rooms toward clutter-free living spaces and fresh air. Appliances like gas stoves, refrigerators, washing machines, and all sorts of electric gadgets—toasters, mixers, irons, vacuum cleaners—were brand new and popular. Similarly, new household products that directly impacted women's work were emerging, from cleansers to processed foods to fabrics.

Many corporations of this era—not just food manufacturers—turned to domestic scientists to develop and test new products. One notable partnership was between Corning Glass Works and Dr. Lucy Maltby. In 1929, Maltby demonstrated the domestic applications for the company's new Pyrex glass. Showing off its attributes as oven safe, relatively unbreakable, and healthier than metal, she helped the company establish a whole line of immensely popular cookware that remains an industry leader today.

In the 1920s, newspapers were beginning to value the voices and interests of women, and many created specific sections targeting them as an audience. Commonly known as the "Women's Pages," these weekly or daily sections evolved to cover many of the issues under the domestic science umbrella. Later, newspapers would offer specialized sections for food, health, fashion, consumer advocacy, gossip and celebrity news, lifestyles, and home design, but in the beginning, all these issues were the beat of the Women's Pages editor.

Newspapers often set up test kitchens and reporters assumed the role of domestic scientist, creating and testing recipes and evaluating new products. Some publications, like *Good Housekeeping* and *Parents' Magazine*, made such a program the centerpiece of their work. Starting in 1900, the Good Housekeeping Experiment Station, later renamed the Good Housekeeping Institute, tested food items and other household products for quality. If the companies that offered those "quality" products were willing to pay for advertising in the magazine, they garnered the Good Housekeeping Seal of Approval.

Throughout the 1940s and 1950s, Durkee-Mower prominently displayed two marks in its print ads: A circle that read "Tested and Commended by Parents' Magazine Consumer Service Bureau," and an oval with "Guaranteed by Good Housekeeping. Replacement or Refund of Money if Not as Advertised."

✦

If Fannie Farmer introduced marshmallow cream to kitchens, Marjorie Mills, a trailblazer for women in newspapers and radio, ensured that Marshmallow Fluff was the brand of choice. Born Marjorie Meader Burns in Maine in 1892, Mills got her start as a general reporter at the *Waterville Morning Sentinel*. She had bigger goals in mind, however, and moved to Boston in her early twenties. She rented a room at the Franklin Square House, a hotel in the South End for young working women, toiling at a munitions factory and as a waitress, all the while

Retailers and manufacturers alike could always count on Marjorie Mills drawing a crowd. *Courtesy Durkee-Mower.*

sending the *Boston Herald Traveler* pieces she had written in an attempt to secure a position there. In 1916, the paper finally relented when she convinced the editor to take her on "just for the summer."

As Mills later recalled, "I got some pretty dreadful assignments. I never seemed to get more than a paragraph into the paper." But the quality of her research and people skills turned things around. An article on a picnic in Chinatown led to feature-length, in-depth pieces for the Sunday edition, and lots of interviews. She was given a society column called "Dear Everybody," and through it she connected with Boston's power brokers.

In the 1920s, Mills was promoted to editor of the Women's Pages, where she remained in charge for the next thirty-six years. The Women's Pages included various pieces of social news, such as wedding announcements and club and society updates. Mills acquired a reputation for having the scoop on Bostonians of every stripe. "She knew just about everybody on the Boston scene and could quote specifics on the idiosyncrasies, foibles, strengths, and troubles of each," wrote one of her former colleagues. "Good Lord, what a book I could write," she used to say with a throaty chuckle.

Like so many other women in the media of this time, Mills was corralled away from "hard news" and marginalized. With rare exceptions, women who may have aspired to cover other stories were mostly restricted to this "kitchen door" approach to the world. Journalism as a whole didn't recognize women for the comparable skills and expertise they brought to their work on the "trivial" Women's Pages—even though it was the best-read section after the front page and the comics. It was common for women to cut recipes from the paper and save their favorite clippings within the covers of a cookbook or inside envelopes or tins. But in these sections, as they extended advice and information, female journalists were also tackling significant issues far ahead of their time, like poverty, addiction, and domestic violence.

Like other editors of Women's Pages, Mills also authored and edited cookbooks. She was responsible for the 1926 *Better Homes Recipe Book* and the 1929 *Home-Makers Guide*, both published by the *Boston Herald Traveler*. When families struggled to provide meals during the hard times of the Depression and World War II, the Women's Pages wrote about poverty and nutrition. (Under an imprint of Houghton Mifflin Company, Mills cheerily wrote the recipe collection *Cooking on a Ration or Food is Still Fun.*)

In 1926, already well known for her role at the *Herald Traveler*, Mills was a regular guest for the WNAC radio show called *The Women's Club.* Mills wasn't the first person you'd consider for radio—she had a gravelly voice with a Maine twang—but it served her well. As radio became more crowded with female hosts, Mills' distinct voice helped her to stand out and build a connection with her audience as someone authentic and relatable.

Later that decade, when the *Boston Herald Traveler* established a formal relationship with WBZ radio, Mills hosted a regionally syndicated show called *New England Kitchen of the Air* three afternoons a week. At the end of the 1930s and into the 1940s, she moved from WBZ over to WNAC and then to Yankee Network for a show of her own called *The Marjorie Mills Hour,* where she could take on whatever issues she chose. Like the hosts of other women's shows of the era, she talked about fashion, food, current events, and more. At the end of that run in the 1950s, Mills was on to a new venture: cohosting a regional radio show with Carl de Suze on WBZ called *Window on the World*, which ran for seventeen years. Among her guests were many contemporary, prominent women including Jacqueline Kennedy.

To her readers and listeners across New England, Marjorie Mills was a teacher, mentor, and friend. Like the other women who took on the mantle of "domestic science expert," Mills leveraged her position as a trusted authority into the world of product endorsements. Indeed, Mills was particularly adept at lining up sponsors. She endorsed Marshmallow Fluff as well as a large and varied group of domestic products, including Maltex Cereal, Johnson's Liquid Floor Wax, Tetley Tea, Doeskin Dinner Napkins, King Arthur Flour, Nestlé Chocolate Chips, and Friend's Baked Beans. She took a shrewd business approach to her relationships with her radio sponsors. Reportedly, when one company was unable to keep up with their advertising commitment during the Depression, she continued the sponsorship relationship in exchange for stock, a gamble that paid off handsomely later.

She featured endorsed products on her radio show and then, amidst

Marjorie Mills gets ready for one of her in-store appearances.
Courtesy Durkee-Mower.

bright displays of the arrayed products, appeared at area stores where she met shoppers face-to-face. Always wearing one of her signature hats, festooned with an assortment of silk flowers or a dramatic pheasant feather, Mills drew large, affectionate crowds of women eager to meet her. Among the archives at Durkee-Mower are images of Mills during these live appearances. She stands before a collection of endorsed products, the store mobbed with women vying for her attention. Mills is easy to spot with her hat popping above the crowd.

In a 1951 edition of the *Boston Herald Traveler* was a three-quarter-page advertisement cross promoting Fluff with Mills' radio show, highlighting the six radio stations across New England where readers could listen in—from Hartford to Springfield, Boston to Bangor. A big photo showed Mills spooning Fluff into a mixing bowl with the declaration, "Marjorie Mills: New England's Foremost Home Economist endorses Fluff." A quote from Mills read, "When I use marshmallow in my own cooking, I always buy FLUFF, the brand I know is pure... the brand experience has proven best for flavor and all-around goodness."

Endorsements such as these led many to critique the Women's Pages and their editors, finding them to be too cozy with advertisers. This was a legitimate concern, especially with cash-strapped local publications and radio shows. For example, it was common for Durkee-Mower's advertising agency to distribute a selection of identical seasonal recipes with press-ready images to dozens of newspapers. (The newspaper editors received a jar of Fluff as well, should they wish to test the recipe themselves.) Many publications established rules requiring published recipes to omit brand names, but busy editors scrambling to fill inches for that day's issue often reprinted the submissions they received verbatim, brand names included. Within a week of Durkee-Mower's mailing such recipes, more than a dozen local papers were running identical articles and images, each of them suggesting a renewal of "time-honored Egg Nog parties" with recipes that called for a Fluff-sweetened beverage. Over the years, this tactic provided Durkee-Mower with regular, wide-reaching, and nearly free promotion.

New Year's Eggnog
by Gretchen McMullen for Durkee-Mower
MAKES 24 CUPS

    4 eggs
    1 jar (7½ ounces) Marshmallow Fluff
    1 tablespoon vanilla
    1 teaspoon orange extract
    2 cups heavy cream
    2 quarts milk
    Ground nutmeg, to taste (optional)

Beat egg yolks and add jar of Marshmallow Fluff, vanilla, and orange extract. Beat to blend. Beat egg whites; whip one cup cream. Fold cream into whites and blend with egg yolk mixture. Add one cup cream and two quarts milk. Chill well. Serve very cold. Sprinkle with ground nutmeg if desired. May be made a day in advance.

Endorsements ran both ways. Women in the media appreciated the boost when their advertisers returned the stamp of approval. Self-serving motives were certainly at play when Durkee-Mower ran a full page advertisement declaring, "All Leading Home Economists Endorse…." along with the names, photos, and affiliations of ten women in the media. Marjorie Mills got top billing in the Durkee-Mower universe, and in this ad her image sat at the top across from Mildred Carson of WBZ and the *Boston Post*. The next level listed Agnes Mahan, household editor at the *Boston Globe*, Mildred Bailey from WCOP, and Louise Morgan, director of women's programs at WNAC radio and WNAC-TV. The third tier held Ruth Mugglebee of the *Boston Record American*, Connie Stackpole of the Granite Network, Christine Evans with *Women's Pages of the Air* on WHDH radio, and poor Susan Mack, so far down the page that her affiliation was accidentally cut off. In a time when the definition

Louise Morgan and Bruce Durkee on WNAC-TV. *Courtesy Durkee-Mower.*

fluff

of a "home economist" or "domestic scientist" was growing increasingly vague and unsubstantiated, just getting into this promotion was a badge of legitimacy. Ultimately, for women in the media, audience numbers and sponsorship dollars measured their success. If a sponsor included you in a full-page advertisement, you had most decidedly arrived. In the case of Mills and Durkee-Mower, the relationship seemed to have developed beyond a business exchange into a professional friendship. Mills was part of several anniversary events at the Fluff factory in the 1950s, standing among the small group of friends and colleagues, a big smile on her face as Fred and Allen cut their annual cake.

Mills overcame the marginalization of women in the media. She achieved financial success with a home on Beacon Hill and two places to summer on Nantucket. Her peers honored her with the Yankee Quill Award through the Society of Professional Journalists and an induction into the Massachusetts Broadcasters Hall of Fame. She was a recognized political powerhouse in the city, too. At a big celebration for her seventieth birthday at the Copley Plaza, Massachusetts Governor John A. Volpe and Mayor of Boston John F. Collins playfully bestowed upon her the title of "Dame Boston."

Even after her retirement in 1966, Mills was known for mentoring young journalists and her active public life. Walking from her home on Pinckney Street, she spent so much time among friends at the Ritz Carlton that she was dubbed "The Den Mother of the Ritz." In her eighties, the hotel hosted an epic birthday party in her honor with a guest list that read like the city's unofficial Social Register. After toasts and tributes, Mills, feeble from arthritis, struggled to stand but kept a dry eye when she declared, "I love you so much, I can't help telling you." Back in her seat, she fluffed her long silk gown, discreetly beckoned a waiter, and muttered, "Get me another scotch."

In a touching, personal tribute upon her passing, the *Boston Globe* columnist Robert Taylor wrote, "She was a wonder and landmark to the very end, and her significance as a pioneer was not lost, though she was inclined to dismiss it, disliking pretension. And she remained to the end also, in every dealing with the world, someone to trust. Her sumptuous flowered hats were an oriflamme."

Trust between customers and this celebrity cast of media-savvy domestic scientists was a powerful marketing tool during this era. Just as Emma Curtis marketed her Snowflake Marshmallow Crème with a personal, authoritative voice, companies wanted to associate themselves with a personality who could further their brands and build unique relationships of confidence. For some companies, the solution was creating a fictional woman to represent their interests.

Enter Betty Crocker. In the 1920s, the Washburn Crosby Company, a flour milling business, created this warm and knowledgeable homemaker to be the standard bearer of the company. In 1924, the Washburn Crosby Company bought a radio station (back when they were easy to come by) and produced *Betty Crocker Cooking School of the Air* with a female announcer reading scripts prepared by the staff of domestic scientists and cooks working in the corporate kitchen. The following year, the program aired on thirteen regional stations, with different women serving as the Betty Crocker voice to each of those audiences. When the National Broadcasting Company (NBC) radio network launched, the fictional Betty Crocker had one of the first shows, a program that continued for twenty-four years.

Durkee-Mower, too, created a fictionalized, idealized homemaker: Lynne White. She never made a radio appearance, but starting in the late 1940s, she was credited as the author of Durkee-Mower's cookbooks. A portrait, reproduced in black-and-white recipe booklets, shows a woman of about thirty with sweetly coiffed blond hair, a white shirt with a Peter Pan collar, and a simple ribbon tie.

In her first appearance in Durkee-Mower's publication, *Fun with Food*, an introductory letter from "Lynne White" presents the book as if she were a company employee scrupulously working away in a test kitchen at the facility. "For a long time now we have been testing and developing recipes using Marshmallow Fluff. And the tempting aromas in our kitchens have been true indicators of the deliciousness of cakes and pies and candies and many other things we have made." She remained the designated author for several editions of the company's *Yummy Book*.

fluff

Playing on the factory's location in Lynn and marshmallow cream's distinctive bright color, the Lynne White moniker is a rather transparent ruse, but this didn't stop letters arriving at the Durkee-Mower offices, addressed to the character and seeking cooking advice. Across five decades, generations of secretaries scratched the signature line of Lynne White at the bottom of letters to consumers, offering cheerful aid and encouragement through the mail, wrapped up with a copy of a *Yummy Book,* or whatever Durkee-Mower swag was available at the time.

Rusty Blazenhoff, a Marshmallow Fluff super fan, wrote to Lynne White in 1996. A native of Cape Cod, Blazenhoff had moved west to California and, while she otherwise enjoyed her new state, she bemoaned it as a Fluff desert. She wrote to Durkee-Mower, inquiring if Lynne White was real because, by her calculations as a lifelong Fluff consumer,

The face of the fictional Lynne White actually belonged to Eleanor Gay, an announcer for the Flufferette radio show on the Yankee Network. Gay's publicity shot (left) was lightly doctored (right) then given to an illustrator, who created a fresh face for Marshmallow Fluff's eternal advocate. *Courtesy Durkee-Mower.*

White's longevity was decidedly suspicious. Blazenhoff further pondered how Durkee-Mower could afford to distribute its recipe books for the modest twenty-five cents and if it was the hippies' obsession with health food that halted distribution of Fluff in the Bay area. She wrapped up her letter with a request for Fluff promotional merchandise as a means to better and more publicly demonstrate her devotion.

Rusty received this letter in reply:

Ms. Blazenhoff:

Congratulations, you are the first writer to have decoded the origin of Lynne White's name. She has been with us for over fifty years, but still maintains her youthful, attractive nature. She has also been fired a few times for some of the letters she has written in reply to customers' complaints that were not favorably received.

I think the only reason that we charge $.25 for the recipe book is that it is too little for the mail department to steal but enough to eliminate those who want a complete freebie. Obviously, it is a losing proposition because the booklet and envelope alone cost nearly $1.00.

Unfortunately, we have no Fluff paraphernalia at this time, but that may change sometime this year.

For your convenience, we are enclosing an order form which you can use to educate some of your California friends. It may be some time before Fluff is distributed there primarily because of the introduction costs.

Thank you for your letter and interests as well.

Yours very truly,
"Lynne White"

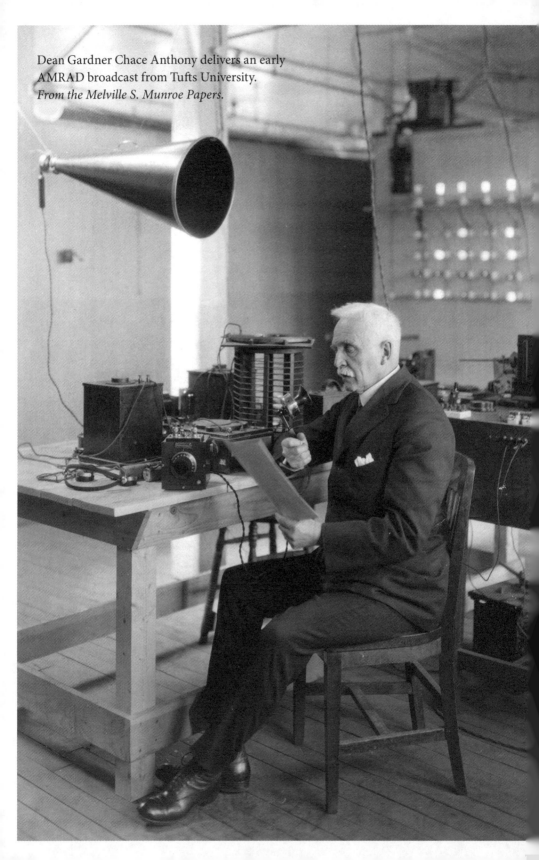

Dean Gardner Chace Anthony delivers an early AMRAD broadcast from Tufts University.
From the Melville S. Munroe Papers.

Pioneers of the Airwaves

AS a fledgling company, Durkee-Mower needed to build brand awareness for Marshmallow Fluff and, like its competitors, relied upon traditional print advertisements in newspapers and magazines to do so. The company's first advertising campaign was in the *Boston Post* in 1926. But print was static, and as delightful as these promotions could be, they were in jeopardy of being lost amidst the clutter of the daily news. What Allen and Fred wanted was something dynamic. Something innovative. Something ambitious, with the power to hold the attention of hundreds of thousands of potential customers. Luckily, there was a new media emerging that could do just the trick: radio.

To coordinate their advertising campaigns, Allen and Fred turned to their childhood friend, Karl Frost. Immediately after World War I, Karl had joined his father's Lynn-based advertising firm, the Harry M. Frost Company. The accounts Karl signed early in his career, like Durkee-Mower, grew into national advertisers, enabling the agency to open a second office in downtown Boston. With Karl serving as vice president and general manager, the Harry M. Frost Company managed its clients' advertising campaigns in newspapers, national magazines, trade papers, and outdoor advertising. Early on, Karl saw the opportunity in radio and he shrewdly pointed his clients in this direction.

fluff

Before World War I, wireless communication was almost exclusively reserved for ships. After the war, however, radio gained appreciation as a means of mass media. In the beginning, radio pioneers were hobbyists, setting up small-scale transmitters and constructing their own receivers. It was a hands-on affair; if you wanted a radio, you built your own. The emphasis was on function rather than style; to an untrained eye, these early receivers looked like junk—just a jumble of wires, a vacuum tube, and a knob stuck on a board. You needed headphones to listen and the sound quality was poor. Interest was limited to those who were technically inclined.

Arguably, the first radio station in the nation as we know them today was based out of the Tufts University campus in Medford. Boston's only radio station until 1922, 1XE (later known as WGI), was a project of the American Radio and Research Corporation (AMRAD).

From their research laboratory and manufacturing space, AMRAD's staff developed radios and their components and produced programming for "the wireless"—an hour or two a few evenings a week. Much like Archibald Query's homemade marshmallow cream, WGI's early offerings were homespun and a modest sideline for the staff at AMRAD. WGI's early transmissions to its small audience were simple. Community volunteers read the news or played phonograph records bartered from a neighborhood record store in exchange for an on-air mention. Meanwhile, AMRAD engineers took on nicknames like Uncle Eddy, who read bedtime stories to the audience. And since pre-recorded music offered such poor sound quality, AMRAD's staff sang and played instruments on air, and whenever possible, area musicians were booked to perform.

Despite the station's small size and meager resources, the radio forerunners at WGI and other similar stations took their programming roles seriously. The airwaves were a shared, public resource; any transmissions should, as such, serve a public purpose. Radio offerings, from the news to entertainment, were expected to be educational, informational, culturally enriching, and—above all—non-commercial.

Within just a few short years, however, radio's landscape changed dramatically. At the start of the 1920s, radio was the purview of amateurs. The transmissions were community produced; the receivers were ready-to-assemble radio kits that AMRAD marketed to boys with an interest in tinkering. By the middle of the decade, however, radio was big business. Thanks to the development of lower-cost vacuum tubes and the introduction of battery power, radio receivers became a widely available consumer product. The machines moved from the workshop to the parlor, set inside decorative cabinetry as a centerpiece for family entertainment. By 1930, radios were in 60 percent of all American homes and radio programming was an essential means of mass communication.

With more and more Americans owning radios, new and existing stations sought to meet the rising demand for programming. In Massachusetts, WGI in Medford expanded broadcasting to seven days a week. WBZ began operating in Springfield in 1921 and then opened a Boston studio in 1924. Edison Electric introduced its station, WEEI, in 1924. WHDH began in Gloucester in 1929. Others started only to eventually close, like WAGS at the Willow Avenue Garage in Somerville, which put out tiny five-watt transmissions. Because there was no government regulation, anyone could start a station, and hundreds—large and small—sprung up across the country.

John Iringle, 14, with the radio he built, 1922.
Courtesy Library of Congress.

Radio receiver manufacturers, like Edison Electric, were bankrolling these stations and their programming, which were still functioning with a non-commercial mandate. Radio retailers soon recognized the opportunity and got into the new media game, too.

One of these visionary retailers was John Shepard III. Shepard's Department Store was at the corner of Winter and Tremont Streets, overlooking the Boston Common opposite the Park Street subway station. Understanding the business opportunities within the new medium, Shepard transformed the entire fourth floor of his family's Boston store into recording studios. In July of 1922, WNAC began broadcasting from there. The Shepard family owned a second store in Providence, Rhode Island, where they launched a companion station, WEAN. With the help of a telephone line, the two stations were able to simulcast programming. Visiting performers with shows at the big theaters and concert halls in Boston or Providence would stop by the stations for a performance and interview to promote their events. The public was welcomed into the downtown stores to watch the live production, see their favorite stars, and—if they didn't already own one—pick up a radio receiver to bring home.

Because radio was expected to be non-commercial, community-led efforts—like at the tiny WAGS studio and WGI—were in a bind. The public's expectations for the quantity and quality of programming were rising. Uncle Eddy's yodeling was no longer good enough. The demands upon announcers, program directors, and producers had grown significant. For a radio show to feature quality musical talent, someone had to find it, schedule it, and secure sponsorships to pay for it. Capitalized stations like Shepard's WNAC were able to hire staff for these tasks; tiny garage stations weren't. The experienced volunteers from community-oriented stations like WGI left to build careers in professional, paid positions.

Though none of the nascent stations were broadcasting for more than a few hours a day, they all needed content to fill their schedules. Radio schedules were broken into ten or fifteen-minute blocks, and businesses commonly reserved one or more of these blocks each week. These sponsors were expected to provide quality programming, tastefully advancing the company's brand through that role. Blatant advertising on what were

Courtesy Durkee-Mower.

meant to be the non-commercial airwaves was heavily frowned upon. The easiest way for companies to walk this tight rope was by sponsoring musical performers using names evocative of their products. For Durkee-Mower, the solution was a musical group called the Flufferettes.

Starting in 1923, Durkee-Mower sponsored a fifteen-minute weekly block of programming on WNAC, a campaign that cost $300 annually—about $4,000 in today's dollars. Joe Rines and his saxophone sextet were the first incarnation of the Flufferettes, performing original songs and popular hits.

Sponsors like Durkee-Mower valued a consistent band name that highlighted their product over a loyalty to specific performers. In fact, it was the radio stations that were expected to engage on-air talent, enlisting a corps of performers, announcers, and producers to present these short programs each week. Over the next three decades, WNAC cast different performers as the Flufferettes, including bands and groups of male and female vocalists.

Yankee Network marquee, 1956. *Courtesy Durkee-Mower.*

Radio isn't a visual medium, but it was a component in this early era. Performances were live, often with studio audiences, and the artists were typically called upon to serve as brand ambassadors for additional, in-person appearances. Visitors to Shepard's Department Store could head up to the fourth floor studios during the Durkee-Mower sponsored time to watch Joe Rines and his band perform as the Flufferettes. Some sponsors dressed their performers in costumes to better emphasize their brands. For example, the Clicquot Club Eskimos, a banjo orchestra sponsored by a ginger ale company, wore fur coats similar to that of the Eskimo boy character who appeared in the product's advertising.

As the decade wore on, the ruse that all this sponsored programming was non-commercial grew harder to maintain. Stations were popping up daily and their competing signals resulted in interruptions and static. The federal government stepped in to impose order in the frenetic radio field.

Through the Federal Radio Commission and the Radio Act of 1927, government licenses designated station call letters and transmission terms for each station so signals would no longer interfere with one another. Even more importantly for businesses like Durkee-Mower, the new category of commercial licensing provided radio stations with a sustainable business model. Commercial radio was born.

As a result of this compromise, radio stations began to merge and affiliate with one another. Two national networks emerged—NBC (National Broadcasting Company) and CBS (Columbia Broadcasting)— while in Boston, the Yankee Network and WBZ became regional leaders. WBZ, previously just a Springfield station, established a second station at Boston's Hotel Bradford on Tremont Street, resulting in a signal that reached across the state. John Shepard III expanded the foothold of WNAC and WEAN, buying up several additional stations and networking with others. Eventually, Shepard's Yankee Network and its twenty-one stations reached audiences through all of New England.

Shepard consolidated his radio operations at the Buckminster Hotel in Kenmore Square. The hotel rooms on the second floor were converted into business offices and audition studios; the ballroom was engaged for live radio performances. This prominent location was later fitted with a bold, illuminated marquee, three stories high, and a street-level display window. Both the marquee and window provided additional

opportunities for the Yankee Network to sell sponsorship space. In 1954, in a broad marketing push, Marshmallow Fluff and the Flufferette show were highlighted in both of these spaces as part of a ten-day campaign.

In the 1930s, Shepard's Yankee Network offered seventeen hours of daily programming, including news, talks by regional political leaders, radio dramas, and sports—including live coverage of Boston Braves and Boston Red Sox baseball and Bruins hockey games. Programs directed toward women and housewives became a particular strength of the Yankee Network. It was here that Marjorie Mills became a household name throughout New England.

Durkee-Mower's early 1920s radio sponsorship was exclusively with WNAC, and the company remained a loyal partner as Shepard's radio empire expanded. Durkee-Mower would continue to sponsor Yankee Network programming through the early 1950s, and when WNAC made the leap to television, Fluff was there too, though more modestly. Over the years, as the Yankee Network's broadcasts stretched farther across New England, Marshmallow Fluff's customer base spread as well.

✦

Durkee-Mower was lucky to have a close rapport with Medford native Joe Rines. Even after becoming a sought-after national performer, he would still return as a special guest on Durkee-Mower-sponsored shows. Born in Boston, Rines performed live in nightclubs in the 1930s and 1940s and made live radio appearances on regional and national stations, including the NBC radio network. He went on to serve as music director of WMCA Radio in New York City and produced national radio programs such as *The Andrews Sisters* and *Colgate Comedy Hour*. Rines was a composer of both big band tunes and commercial jingles. He is credited with promotions for Ajax Cleanser, Halo Shampoo, and Quaker Oats.

Today, Rines may be best known for his role in a renowned instance of censorship. Just a year after the passage of the Hays Code and its censorship of the motion picture industry, radio executives were similarly exercising control over content they feared would lead to accusations of indecency. Lacking any official government regulation, radio program directors and managers exerted their power in so-called purity

fluff

campaigns, where they made an example of performers slipping in double-entendres and saucy lyrics. The sense that radio was a common public ground operating across shared airwaves was still a potent point of view, and programming was expected to be family friendly.

In 1931, Joe Rines was very publicly caught up in one of these moments of industry restrictions when John Clark, program director at WBZ and WBZA, cut off Rines and his band mid-song during a live broadcast. The director deemed the performance of "This is the Missus," a popular upbeat Broadway tune, to be too risqué. Some of the lyrics in question included:

> You've got lots of bumblebees buzzing 'round your honeycomb
> When we're out or at your home
> We've no privacy
> You could put my mind at ease
> Make feel so very proud
> If you'd only tell the crowd
> That you belong to me.
> This is the missus
> Can't look her over
> She's all mine
> I'll get no kisses
> Now I'm in clover
> I've caught some fish on my line.

Rines was indignant. He told the *Springfield Republican*, "It is preposterous to think that a man could write or sing a song about his own wife that had the least bit of suggestive or double meaning."

The event caused a small uproar at the time and is still cited today as evidence of Boston's overzealous conservatism. The truth of the matter is that his industry colleagues—if not Durkee-Mower and the public—were well aware of Joe Rines' alter ego. Under the pseudonym of John Ryan, Rines composed and recorded a number of novelty party songs that gleefully embraced sexual double-entendres, gently sauced by today's standards, with titles such as "I Wish I Were a Fairy" and "The Moustache Song." Rines had quite a few songs in his repertoire that would very legitimately send a program director rushing to the "off" button.

After Rines, many others performed under the name of the Fluffer-ettes over the years. Among them were Horace Heidt and his Brigadiers. This band would go on to have a number one hit in 1937 with a swooning tune called "Gone with the Wind" (not to be confused with the Civil War novel and movie by the same name). In 1938, Heidt topped the charts again with "Ti-Pi-Tin." But it was after his days as a Flufferette that band-leader Heidt—now with His Musical Knights—found his most enduring fame with "The Hut-Sut Song." The 1940s novelty tune has an earworm chorus so intense that it was jokingly declared "a national disease" at the time. By the mid-1930s, the Durkee-Mower-sponsored show included a variety of performers with the Flufferettes name reserved for a trio of female vocalists. With the slogan, "They Supply the Musical Meringue of Radio With Melody That's Sweeter Than Sweet," the Flufferette trio served as consistent performers, flanked by a variety of guests invited to join them each week.

In the winter and spring of 1930, Durkee-Mower expanded its radio show beyond music, sponsoring a series of Sunday evening programs

Joe Rines and his band, 1930. *Courtesy Durkee-Mower.*

on WNAC and WEAN. For twelve weeks, live audiences gathered at the new Yankee Network studios for *Book-of-the-Moment* drama, a radio play with a musical program. The short comedic plays had simple storylines. Loosely tying the series together, each show concluded with the hero, Lowell Cabot Boswell, secretly recording something in a book. At the end of the series, the mystery of what Boswell was writing about was revealed. Surprise! He was recording all the wonderful things you can make with Marshmallow Fluff.

After the investment in the *Book-of-the-Moment* drama series, Durkee-Mower went back to simpler programming. It's unfair to judge the series by today's standards—the writing sure was hokey—but it was most likely a disappointing return on investment that kept the company from trying again. They had started with a radio-advertising budget of just $300 seven years before. In 1930, though, Durkee-Mower spent two hundred times that—$60,000—on radio advertising alone. That's equivalent to about $850,000 today, and a heck of a lot of Fluff to sell.

In the 1940s, the Durkee-Mower sponsored shows featured a trio of singing sisters—Rita, Mary, and Rosemary Gallagher—with a variety of guest soloists performing contemporary pop tunes. Now that radio could be honestly commercial, the Durkee-Mower shows included straightforward product promotions. The announcer pitched Marshmallow Fluff directly: "Be sure to use Fluff in your frostings, sauces, cookies, and candies!" The twenty-second theme song closed out the show, sung by the Flufferette trio and backed by a soothing, echoing xylophone.

> For something delicious
> You know well enough
> You will get your wishes
> With Marshmallow Fluff.
> And each and every serving
> Of this tempting Fluff
> Will bring praise deserving
> Of Marshmallow Fluff.

Decades after the transition to commercial radio, broadcast schedules were still sprinkled with blocks of sponsored programming. Namesake performers continued to promote brands such as Marshmallow Fluff, but their airtime was punctuated with clunky, transparent advertising. Manufacturers appreciated the role these performers played as brand ambassadors, however. As Durkee-Mower wrote in a grocer industry publication, the Flufferettes "convert interest and goodwill into increased purchases over your counters." Eventually the Flufferettes and other sponsored musical acts would become relics, leaving us with just tedious commercials between pop songs.

✦

Durkee-Mower and its promotional team at the Harry M. Frost Company were highly attentive to the company's marketing strategy. During the summer, when Fluff sales typically dipped, Durkee-Mower's radio presence was more limited, usually to just one radio ad during the weekday news programs. During the fall and winter, when the company sought

Flufferettes sing in the WNAC studio, circa 1940s.
Courtesy Lynn Historical Society.

Courtesy Durkee-Mower.

to maximize seasonal sales, the campaigns hit high gear, with promotions that included the Flufferette musical show on the radio as well as a variety of print ads and billboards. The team experimented with time slots for their promotions on the Yankee Network. For a period, the Flufferettes were on the airwaves on Tuesday evenings, then Tuesday afternoons. In the late 1940s, they tried lunchtime. In the 1950s, reflective of changing shopping and listening patterns, Fluff was featured on the morning edition of Yankee Network News. But the very best time slot, and one that Fluff claimed throughout most of the 1940s, was Sunday at 6:45 p.m., when families gathered around the radio to hear the biggest national show of the era: *The Ed Sullivan Show*.

Before he gained acclaim on television, Ed Sullivan was a radio star. In 1950, when Sullivan made the transition to television with *Toast of the Town*, sponsored by the Lincoln-Mercury car company, Sullivan brought his show on the road, traveling across the country to sites like Boston's Opera House.

Since Sullivan's show aired on WNAC radio's companion television channel, Durkee-Mower leveraged its Yankee Network relationship and took Sullivan's live appearance as an opportunity for cross-promotional advertising. In a large newspaper advertisement, Sullivan's weekly television show, its sponsor, his live Boston appearance, and an endorsement of Fluff were tidily brought together. Below a large photo of a young Ed Sullivan, "America's No. 1 TV Master-of-Ceremonies," was his endorsement of Marshmallow Fluff: "You all know Mercury gives you a smooth ride—but for smooth eating, you should try Marshmallow FLUFF! Next time you're watching TV, take my tip for a jiffy snack. Spread some crackers with FLUFF and jelly or peanut butter! Delicious! Top 'em off with a steaming cup of rich, satisfying SWEECO—and you'll see what I mean. Man, that's real eating pleasure!"

Bruce Durkee flew fighter planes over the Pacific during
World War II. During the war, Durkee-Mower gave away
flying ace pins to promote Fluff and to quietly honor Bruce.
Courtesy Durkee-Mower.

Wartime and
the Business of Fluff

THE Great Depression was a challenging time for many businesses, but Durkee-Mower was doing relatively well. Government price controls were giving profits a squeeze, but sales were strong. Thanks to Karl Frost, the Flufferettes, and Marjorie Mills, the demand for Marshmallow Fluff was robust—and this delicious concoction was making its way into increasingly more New England kitchens. Fred and Allen's families were financially secure, and they did what they could to contribute to others in need.

Community engagement overall was high in this era. In fact, associations and clubs of every sort—social, political, and athletic—saw their highest levels of participation between the two world wars. Allen and Fred took on leadership roles in numerous community organizations, which served both their business and personal interests. After World War I, both men enlisted in the National Guard, were sworn members of the Masonic Ionic Club of Swampscott, and active on the Board of Directors of the Lynn Boys Club. Allen was also president of the Lynn Rotary Club, a member of the Chamber of Commerce, and trustee for the Five Cents Savings Bank. Despite all these commitments, Fred and his wife found time to be part of local theaters, and Allen, who was commodore of the Swampscott Yacht Club among other activities, taught sailing to other club members and raced boats from Boston to Bermuda.

To boost morale during the trying years of the late 1930s and early 1940s, Durkee-Mower sponsored teams for men's basketball and base-ball and women's basketball and softball. All the teams were technically called Durkee-Mower's Flufferettes, though the men's teams were of-ten given the more "masculine" nickname of the Swampscott Fluffs or the Durkee-Mowers. With basketball in winter and baseball and soft-ball in summer, the teams generally played twice a week in the North Shore Leagues against city-allied teams sponsored by other business-es, churches, and clubs. Their competitors included the Friends' Box Team of Danvers, the Sporties of Lynn (under the sponsorship of Lynn Sporting Goods,) the Beverly Girls Club, the Arrowettes of Saugus, and the Melley Club of Revere. Walter Butler, a former welterweight boxing champion of New England who had taken up a new career manufactur-ing cigars, sponsored the Butler Pals of Chelsea, a men's baseball team. General Electric, with a site in Lynn, had several teams for East Lynn. Players, aged in their teens and twenties, included (but were not limited to) employees of the sponsoring company.

✦

For companies that had been limping though the Depression, the Great New England Hurricane of 1938 marked their death knell. While Durkee-Mower sustained some flooding, direct impact on the business was minimal. In fact, as Allen and Fred often did, they looked toward the future to secure their business.

Though it launched in 1920, it wasn't until 1938 that Fred and Allen officially incorporated the company, ratifying Allen as president, Fred as treasurer, and Charles Jenkins and Chester Rich as vice presidents. They held these titles loosely, however. In practice, Durkee-Mower functioned as a partnership between Fred and Allen, with Jenkins and Rich as supporting players.

After just eight years at the Brookline Avenue location in Lynn, Durkee-Mower already needed more room to meet the demand for ever more Fluff and Sweeco—and to add new products. Fred and Allen scouted out a location on Paradise Road in Swampscott but town reg-ulations no longer allowed manufacturing use of the site. The appeals process moved slowly and the company considered alternatives.

Meanwhile, Durkee-Mower turned to safeguarding its key assets: its brand names. Since patenting its recipes or production processes was not an option, Durkee-Mower looked to the one legal protection af-forded to the company: trademark. Before World War II, most small companies did not trademark brand names, deeming it unnecessary. Even if companies sought to do so, the trademark process was anything but straightforward. It wasn't until 1946, when interest in such legal protections surged, that the federal government passed the Langham Act, which outlined the procedures for trademark registration.

The primary way to claim a trademark is through active use rather than intention. Durkee-Mower had been using the Marshmallow Fluff name since it founded its company in 1920 and, through that use, had

The Flufferettes basketball players pose for a team photo, Lynn, 1940.
Courtesy Durkee-Mower.

claimed a trademark; the paperwork was just a formality. As the company's branding was brought together, Durkee-Mower took the opportunity to rename its instant cocoa mix. Before 1938, the product was known as Durkee-Mower's Instant Sweet Milk Cocoa. After 1938, it would be forever known as Sweeco. (At least until production ceased in the 1960s.)

When Durkee-Mower petitioned the federal government for official recognition of its brands, however, the required public notice of its application brought forth an unsettling discovery. The Limpert Brothers company, a New Jersey-based manufacturer of ice cream toppings, was using the same Marshmallow Fluff name.

The two companies scrambled, researching who could rightly claim precedent. Until this moment, Allen and Fred had minimized Archibald's contribution, touting Valentine's Day 1920 as the company's inauguration date. Locked in a contest with the Limpert Brothers, however, Durkee-Mower now needed to reach back in time as far as it could to before the launch of its partnership to document when its Marshmallow Fluff brand was first sold.

A sixty-five-year-old Archibald Query was probably not much help. Archibald had moved numerous times in the intervening years and, beyond nostalgia, there would have been little need to preserve the records of a product he'd stopped selling two decades prior. Not to mention that Archibald's "manufacturing" of Marshmallow Fluff had been a modest enterprise with none of the marks of a formal business such as print advertisements. According to Archibald's family, there may have been some resentment, too. Archibald and Lizzy were facing a paltry retirement. The Great Depression had been a struggle, knocking Archibald out of work for months at a time. A generation later, seeing the success of Durkee-Mower, the Archibald family was quietly disgruntled, wishing Archibald had cut a better deal.

With limited documentation available from Archibald, Fred and Allen were in a pickle. Given all this, Durkee-Mower eventually asserted a start date of 1917. It's unknown what evidence Durkee-Mower presented to substantiate the claim, but it's likely it played the only card it had: the advent of the electric mixer—and when that equipment would have been available to Archibald—because there is no way anyone could make marshmallow cream without the aid of such a machine.

But it wasn't enough. The Limpert Brothers bettered Durkee-Mower, claiming 1910 as the premiere of its Marshmallow Fluff, presenting print evidence of the product among its advertised line of confections in 1913. Though neither company had formally registered the trademark, the Limpert Brothers precedent won the day. The name of Marshmallow Fluff was rightly theirs.

How did the overlapping brands continue unknown to each other for nearly two decades despite the juggernaut of Durkee-Mower's advertising? One important reason was that the Limpert Brothers' Fluff had a completely different customer base than Durkee-Mower's Marshmallow Fluff. Limpert Brothers Fluff, like all its syrups, bases, fruit, and sauces, was sold exclusively to food service establishments—soda fountains, restaurants, and hotels—to be used as an ice cream topping. While Durkee-Mower was marketing to the general public, Limpert Brothers exclusively approached businesses. The product itself had different properties. Able to cascade softly from a ladle, Limpert Brothers Fluff had a softer texture than Durkee-Mower's, which is stiffer, stickier, and sometimes maddeningly difficult to separate from a knife or bread. Since it was never sold in stores, Limpert Brothers packaged its product in large, simple cans with a minimum of design finesse.

From Durkee-Mower's perspective, maintaining the name was essential. All those years and dollars spent on expensive radio and print advertising, promotional events and sports team sponsorships, billboards and packaging design, all that investment was to establish the name of Marshmallow Fluff, and Marshmallow Fluff alone, as the name to trust. If Durkee-Mower didn't have claim to the name, all was lost.

Limpert Brothers had nothing to lose and everything to gain. For its wholesale buyers and distributors, as long as the price and product were the same, "Marshmallow Fluff" was just a descriptor in the Limpert catalog. The soda jerks didn't care what name was on the can of marshmallow topping they dumped into the dispenser. The kids eating sundaes covered in soupy marshmallow cream didn't even know there was a name or brand.

It would have been relatively easy for Limpert Brothers to discover how much Durkee-Mower had invested in its brand name. Marshmallow Fluff was the number one marshmallow cream in New England.

Without the name, Durkee-Mower would be starting over, just another tin among a small sea of marshmallow cream. Limpert Brothers held all the cards.

From the Durkee-Mower perspective, Limpert Brothers demanded an exorbitant amount to sell the trademark. There was no way Durkee-Mower could possibly come up with that kind of cash. To refuse the deal, though, would spell disaster. The team at Durkee-Mower put their heads together and, in a stroke of genius, came up with an innovative idea.

Allen offered John Limpert one-fifth the amount he demanded. In exchange, the two companies would share the name. The proposal would allow Durkee-Mower to continue to use the Marshmallow Fluff name but exclusively for a product marketed to the "retail grocery customer." Under the deal, Durkee-Mower would restrict sales in new markets. Outside of New England, Durkee-Mower's Marshmallow Fluff could only be sold in containers sixteen ounces or smaller. Limpert Brothers could continue selling its marshmallow ice cream topping in bulk with no restrictions whatsoever.

The two companies ratified this unique arrangement in 1939 and have honored it to this day. In the ensuing years, formal trademark sharing arrangements such as these have been legally disallowed. While the gentlemen's agreement still stands, the federal government lists Durkee-Mower as the sole owner of the Marshmallow Fluff trademark.

Though the neighborhood soda fountains are long gone and the popularity of marshmallow ice cream toppings has waned, the Limpert Brothers company continues to produce Marshmallow Fluff. By all evidence, the company is limping along, its best days well behind it. Despite doing little to build it, Limpert Brothers extols its claim to the Marshmallow Fluff name, declaring prominently on its website, "Our trademark Marshmallow Fluff is one of the oldest and best known brands in America. Over nine decades of food service, distributors, people in hotels, resorts, casinos, restaurants, diners, sundae ice cream shops, hospitals, nursing homes, ice cream or yogurt manufacturers and as well, the general public, have known or used our trademark Marshmallow Fluff." The website layers the unearned bravado thickly, "In fact, our trademark, Marshmallow Fluff, must be known to almost everyone who has ever had a child, raised a child, was related to a child, befriended a child, or was a child."

For its part, Durkee-Mower remains stoically silent on the subject. Moving forward, the counting of anniversaries (and what number to put on the ever-present cake) became muddled, as the founders jockeyed between marking the birth of their star product and the year Fred and Allen began their business. While 1920, the inaugural year of their partnership, remained an important marker for them, after settling the case, Durkee-Mower shrewdly changed its promotional materials to read, "Marshmallow Fluff Since 1917."

✦

Mere months after Durkee-Mower settled the trademark crisis, World War II began. The blow to Durkee-Mower was immediate despite the fact that the US military had yet to enter the conflict. Veterans Fred and Allen were shaken. Allen's eldest son, Bruce, was turning seventeen, and the fathers were fearful of what lay ahead. Inside the factory, they had to scramble as the government stockpiled tin. In a flash, the metal can that Durkee-Mower used to package Fluff for the past twenty years was gone, and the company was forced to quickly switch to a glass jar with a paper label. Changing the packaging was no simple task; it was shipping four million containers of Fluff each year. After America officially declared war, Durkee-Mower patriotically pitched this new container as the "Liberty Glass Jar."

Through 1941, as Europe erupted, sorrows came in quick succession. The team of four was cut in half. Fred's father-in-law and Durkee-Mower Vice President Charles Jenkins died at the age of seventy-seven. Just months later, Chester Rich died at the age of fifty-seven. That horrible year closed with the worst news yet: Japan bombed Pearl Harbor and the United States was fighting another world war on two fronts.

At the close of the 1942 Flufferette men's baseball season, Fred and Allen invited the team to dinner at the Tedesco Country Club. It was intended to be an upbeat celebration but the conversation turned solemn despite their efforts. All anyone could talk about was what lay ahead. Many of the boys had already enlisted and were awaiting deployment, and others were preparing to go. As they pondered the possibility of playing together the following summer, all silently knew the answer. Allen and Fred each gave a brief speech, thanking the group for their fair play and wishing them well, bemoaning "the little guy with the mustache" who had changed their lives. One by one, the players took turns toasting the team and declaring their resolve to see the war quickly through, each struggling to maintain a stiff upper lip. As the group parted with long hugs and handshakes, they promised to gather again after the war—but that was the end of Flufferette sports.

Like the men who played for the Fluff teams, the Flufferette women athletes did their part for the war effort. Female players like Rose Marie McGoldrick Ryan joined the Civil Air Patrol, a civilian auxiliary of the United States Air Force. She was among the crews tasked with spotting the German U-boats active up and down America's East Coast.

History repeated itself in the Durkee family as Bruce—like his father before him—withdrew from his college studies to go to war. Bruce served as a US Navy carrier pilot and was stationed in the South Pacific, where he flew a Torpedo Bomber. Later, when Allen's middle son, Don, came of age he enlisted, too.

Bruce Durkee during World War II. *Courtesy Durkee-Mower.*

Two young men working at the Durkee-Mower factory entered the service early in the war. Then, in 1943, the employees gathered again to see off three more young men. Armand Beatrice, Charles Palleshi, and William Benevento, all nineteen, joined the navy. After a special lunch in the factory and a group portrait with their Fluff family, each received the gift of a fountain pen from their fellow employees and cash from the company with best wishes for their speedy and safe return.

Throughout the war, Fred and Allen reached out to reassure these young men serving abroad. It was somber encouragement, seasoned by their experience in the twenty-sixth division. One of the handwritten letters they received in return, dispatched from Sicily, is preserved in the company's archives:

> Dear Dinty and Joe,
>
> Gee, fellas, I was tickled to death with both your letters. I am so darn busy now I just haven't time to thank you each in a separate letter, so here goes. I thought Africa was bad, but you should see this country. Dirty people starving and full of bugs. I have more bites on my body than a dog fleas. (I believe they are flea bites.) Well, it looks as though we are still going to stay in the thick of it. All the troops are seasoned from the Africa wars. They can keep the 26th home to parade for the girls. The boys over here deserve a lot of credit. They've been working day and night. At home we were bothered a bit by Jerry [a nickname used by the Allies for the Germans], but he is on the defensive now. It is a year today overseas. That seems like a long time. I know both you guys spent 18 months in the last. Well, I must close. Best of luck to you both and to your families.

✦

In December of 1941, right after the bombing at Pearl Harbor, the government quickly passed a number of regulations to ensure adequate supplies of major commodities for the war effort. Through the War

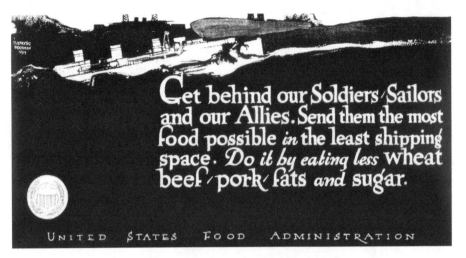

Get behind our Soldiers, Sailors and our Allies. Send them the most food possible *in* the least shipping space. *Do it by eating less* wheat beef, pork, fats *and* sugar.

UNITED STATES FOOD ADMINISTRATION

Courtesy Library of Congress.

Production Board, the federal government tightened access to raw sugar and determined the distribution of refined sugar, giving priority to the production of armaments and military provisions. M-55 was the specific regulation governing small food producers like Durkee-Mower. No one knew how long the war would last or what to expect in terms of incoming sugar supplies; the regulation did not set clear expectations, other than to say that sugar would be limited.

Allen and Fred were worried. Grocers' shelves were empty of Fluff, and Durkee-Mower couldn't give any assurances on when orders would be filled. Between holiday baking with Fluff and the cold months demanding Sweeco, the winter was always Durkee-Mower's busiest time. As servicemen deployed, families needed Fluff for care packages. Durkee-Mower orders were at an all-time high. It needed sugar, and it needed it fast.

Durkee-Mower sent an appeal to the federal government in early January but received a denial only days later. It was collegial but clear. Durkee-Mower, like other manufacturers, would receive sugar allotments based on a percentage of its 1941 sales. Despite the company's projections for continued strong growth in 1942, despite the clear wartime spike in demand, despite the potential layoffs as staff stood idle, the government wasn't making any exceptions. The letter from the Office of Production Management (OPM) clarified that the federal order "does not provide for unusual expansion of an individual organization." The OPM continued, "It is the objective of the Office of Production Management to administer M-55 and amendments as equitably as possible. We feel sure that you will make every reasonable effort to avoid unemployment in your organization, although it does not appear that any exemptions can be granted you at this time."

Out of luck, Durkee-Mower addressed an open letter "To the Trade":

> We wanted to write you weeks ago, but frankly, until today had nothing but rumors on which to base our course.
>
> We wrote to the O.P.M. in Washington on January 12th appealing for relief on sugar, and just received the enclosed copy today from A. H. Bowman, Chief, Sugar Section O.P.M., Washington D.C. The Boston office of the O.P.M. have been most cooperative and have given worthwhile assistance with no avail.
>
> You can readily see from their letter, that for us to maintain equitable distribution of Marshmallow Fluff and Sweeco, we will be required to distribute these products on the same basis as we are permitted to purchase our raw materials.
>
> If, for example, we can purchase sugar based on a PERCENTAGE of our 1941 consumption, to continue our policy of fair treatment, we will be forced to sell Marshmallow Fluff and Sweeco to you based on a PERCENTAGE of your 1941 purchases.
>
> Please write to us if you have any better suggestions.
>
> Yours very truly,
> DURKEE-MOWER INC.

Like other manufacturers in a similar predicament, Durkee-Mower engaged the Flufferettes to make the best of a bad situation. Under normal circumstances any company would try to maximize consumption; Durkee-Mower's advice was now to slow sales and to spread the precious Fluff as thin as possible. During radio spots, the announcer would recite statements such as these:

fluff

Our government has asked us to conserve food. There are many ways of doing this. One is by not wasting the available food we have. Another is to buy only for present needs such foods as eggs, butter or milk. These two methods can be used to conserve the supply of MARSHMALLOW FLUFF - the light, creamy marshmallow. FLUFF like butter, eggs or milk - it's better when fresh, and should not be stored for a long time. So buy only one jar at a time and use it wisely. Stretch the supply by diluting FLUFF with water to make a smooth, creamy marshmallow sauce ideal as a topping for puddings, baked apples, apple sauce or gelatines. --- Grocers throughout New England are receiving regular amounts of MARSH-MALLOW FLUFF - but many times their supply is limited - so please have patience and wait for a new stock to arrive.

Simultaneously, Durkee-Mower worked to keep its brokers happy. Brokerages and sales people sold Marshmallow Fluff on commission to chains and individual grocery stores. Limited Fluff sales directly cut their revenue. In 1942 Durkee-Mower sent the following correspondence to National Brokerage Company:

All we can say at this time is that we deeply appreciate the attitude of our many good friends in the grocery trade for their kind cooperation and acceptance of our being forced to supply Fluff and Sweeco on a quota basis. Please be assured that Durkee-Mower will not in any way abuse this faith the trade has shown in our policy to treat all equitably and to serve each and everyone to the best of our ability under these war conditions. Under no conditions will we change our formula in an attempt to stretch our raw materials, and the high quality of our products will meet the standards maintained for over a period of twenty years.

As had been the case in World War I, the major manufacturers of candy bars and other sweets maintained healthy business with large and growing military contracts to fulfill. These companies had access to sugar but were required to divert it for government commissioned production. These candy producers similarly encouraged their customers to remain patient when supplies were running low, with the added twist that the treats were needed for the troops. A 1943 advertisement in *Life Magazine* from the Curtiss Candy Company reads, "Occasionally some dealers may temporarily be out of Baby Ruth or Butterfinger. If you don't find them on the counter one day... look again the next. We're doing our best to fill domestic orders.... but with us, as with every patriotic American, the boys in service have first call."

The US government didn't use rationing because there was a lack of domestic sugar. Rationing was a tool to determine sugar's distribution. In actuality, America was awash in sugar and Americans had never before manufactured and consumed so many sweets. By the end of the war, six thousand confectioners had churned out 2.8 billion pounds of candy, and annual consumption in the United States reached an all-time high of 20.5 pounds per capita.

For Durkee-Mower and other manufacturers, commercial sugar rationing wasn't the only wartime problem. Gasoline was tough to come by, too. Enterprises like the Callerman Pony Express picked up the task by enlisting traditional horses and wagons. "No Gas - So What - We Cover the Trade," it proclaimed. Callerman worked with manufacturers and grocers to distribute a disjointed assortment of foodstuffs, including Marshmallow Fluff, Malto Meal, Comet Rice, peanuts and pecans, and shrimp and oysters.

As the war went on, the government implemented price controls to combat inflation and profiteering. Durkee-Mower monitored these reports and adjusted accordingly. In April of 1943, Allen issued this letter to grocers:

Gentlemen:

Since May 4, 1942 Marshmallow Fluff has been invoiced to the trade at $1.85 per dozen for the 9 oz. jar "subject to change until maximum price is established under Section 3 (b) of the General Maximum Price Regulations". All invoices were endorsed with the above quotation.

We have, as of April 10, 1943, been notified that our maximum price is now $1.75 a dozen and we are now requested to notify each customers that your computations on the basis of $1.85 should be discounted as of this day. Your selling price should be recomputed on the basis of our authorized price of $1.75.

A check for the difference between $1.85 and $1.75 on all your purchases of 9 oz. glass jars from May 4, 1942 to date will be sent you as soon as possible.

Very truly yours,
Durkee-Mower Inc.
H. Allen Durkee

The Callerman Pony Express steps up in hard times, circa 1944. *Courtesy Durkee-Mower.*

Stateside, Durkee-Mower did what it could to support the war effort. When Fluff production stopped due to restrictions on sugar, the staff wrapped electronics in waterproof packaging to send overseas for the military. When fundraising events needed entertainers, Durkee-Mower sent in the Flufferettes. One of the biggest of these performances was an all-star rally for the Greater Boston United War Fund in 1942. A crowd of twenty thousand attendees packed the Boston Garden to support the American Red Cross, the Greater Boston Community Fund, and various soldier and sailor service groups. The Flufferettes were a good draw, but the headliners of the show were America's darlings, Mickey Rooney and his new bride, starlet Ava Gardner.

The company also demonstrated patriotism in broad, general ways, like adding the slogan "Buy War Bonds" on many of its print ads. In a promotion perhaps inspired by Bruce's role flying over the Pacific, Durkee-Mower offered special aviation pins to young customers. "Send for 'Your Wings of the Air' Today," the ad proclaimed. Kids who sent in ten cents and two small Fluff labels or one large Fluff label received a gold-plated, twenty-two-karat aviation pin. The gender roles of the time were heavily reinforced: "Boys! You'll be proud to wear a pin similar to insignias worn by ace army and navy fliers." And: "It's a Beauty! Girls! Get a smart wings pin like airline hostesses wear."

✦

February of 1945 marked Durkee-Mower's silver anniversary, but Allen and Fred were not in celebratory moods. Despite strong progress by the Allies, victory was not quite at hand. Bruce and Don remained in harm's way, and they had learned that Armand Beatrice, one of the young men from the shipping department, was killed in Italy just ten months after enlisting.

The thirty employees of Durkee-Mower decided to organize a surprise event for their bosses to mark the milestone. They catered a dinner on the factory floor. At the head table, Allen and Fred's wives sported festive corsages beside their husbands and the senior staff. After the meal and the traditional cake, the employees presented their bosses with a barometer, a signal that better days were surely ahead. Perhaps to encourage

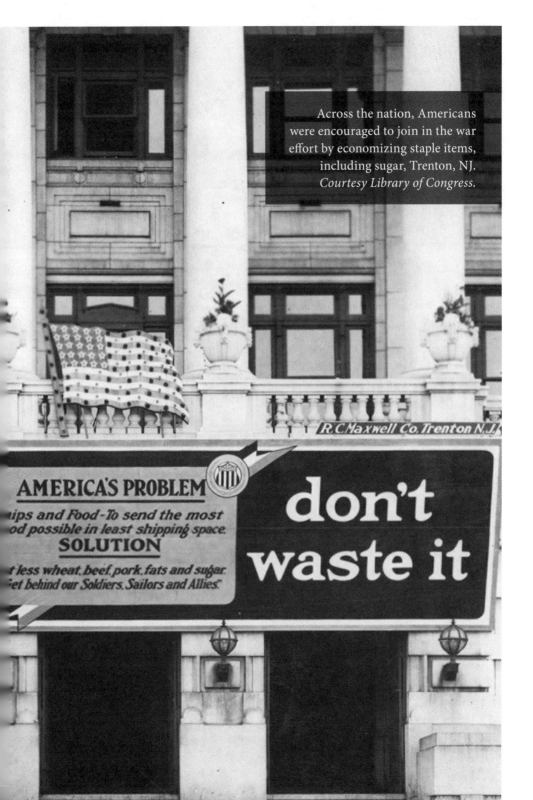

Across the nation, Americans were encouraged to join in the war effort by economizing staple items, including sugar, Trenton, NJ. *Courtesy Library of Congress.*

R.C. Maxwell Co. Trenton N.J.

AMERICA'S PROBLEM

ships and Food—To send the most food possible in least shipping space.

SOLUTION

Eat less wheat, beef, pork, fats and sugar. Get behind our Soldiers, Sailors and Allies.

don't waste it

Factory portrait, 1945. *Courtesy Durkee-Mower.*

themselves as much as their staff, Fred and Allen assured their team that the company remained strong. They pledged that the expansion planned in 1937 would come. A new and larger plant was in their future, just as soon as the war was over.

Unfortunately, Fred and Allen couldn't quite keep their promise. Though the war in Europe officially ended that summer and Japan surrendered later that year, a return to business as usual was still far off—at least for Durkee-Mower. Building materials, equipment, and even the basic ingredients for Fluff were still restricted, putting operations in peril.

In the spring of 1947, nearly two full years after the war ended, sugar supplies remained low at Durkee-Mower. Without adequate materials, the factory line would stumble to a halt. To deal with the crisis, Karl brokered a deal with colleagues working in the manufacture of another home-grown Massachusetts food: cranberries. In April of 1947, Allen wrote a letter to Marcus Urann of Cranberry Canners, Inc. in South Hanson, Massachusetts. "We honestly believe that sugar controls will be withdrawn by fall, and this loan has permitted us to carry-on in a very trying period which we are going through now. As Karl has told you, the market is being flooded with many brands of marshmallow. Where they get the sugar we do not know, but no one in Washington or locally can tell us the answer as to why new concerns can get all the sugar they want, and go around to the trade offering unlimited amounts of marshmallow while we are still being rationed..."

Even though sugar rationing continued, Durkee-Mower was able to maintain adequate supplies after that. It celebrated with a price break its wholesale customers.

> For nearly thirty years one of the important policies of this company is to operate and sell our products at a fair price commensurate with a reasonable profit.
>
> Although we are still unable to supply all the FLUFF that you want, we have increased production, due to larger sugar allotments, which affects a savings in manufacturing costs which we are pleased to pass on to you.
>
> Consequently, we are reducing the price of Marshmallow FLUFF effective as of Monday, May 19th.

By midsummer, Durkee-Mower's sugar woes were officially over. On July 28, 1947, a secretary took a phone message on a commonplace pink "While You Were Out" slip. It is the only phone message in one hundred years of Marshmallow Fluff history that has been preserved. It indicates that Mr. Waldo of Revere Sugar called. Without the exclamation points it most certainly deserved, the message simply reads: "Industrial Sugar Rationing ended at noon today."

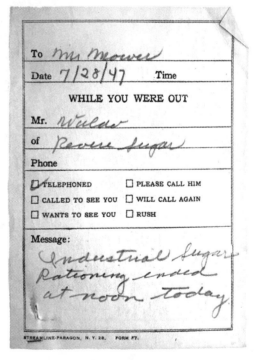

Courtesy Durkee-Mower.

139

Inside the factory, circa 1940s.
Courtesy Durkee-Mower.

Thoroughly Modern Fluff

IN 1950, Durkee-Mower marked its thirtieth anniversary by finally realizing those 1937 factory expansion plans. Now tripled in size to thirty thousand square feet, at a cost of $200,000 (roughly $2 million today), Durkee-Mower had plenty of room for all the company's functions—production, offices, materials storage, a shipping area, even a proper break room.

In 1936, Durkee-Mower had purchased the property running parallel to the railroad on Brookline Avenue to the corner of Empire Street in Lynn. The parcel included the factory acquired through the merger with Rich's Instant Cocoa, as well as several garages where other businesses stored and repaired cars. Due to delays caused by the Great Depression and then World War II, it wasn't until 1945 that Durkee-Mower could finally began to expand its facilities.

In the mid-1940s, the original factory continued operations unimpeded as the company built a two-story building for its administrative offices on the corner of Empire Street. When construction materials became more readily available in the late 1940s, the old garages were demolished and a new manufacturing facility was constructed in the middle, creating an interconnected three-building complex. Designed by Gilbert Small and Company of Boston and built by William Bailey

Company, the new facilities thoughtfully included specialized areas for whipping, filling, capping, and packing Marshmallow Fluff. The old factory was now primarily reserved for storage space.

Building OUR FUTURE NOW!

Construction has started on our new modern plant to provide for post war increased production of—
Marshmallow Fluff and Sweeco.

Our new plant has a seven-car siding for loading and unloading, which will enable us to handle 300 cars per year.

Our new manufacturing kitchens will have complete humidity and temperature control. They will be windowless kitchens, electrically filtered, assuring pure air at all times—with plenty of sunlight through glass brick walls. All manufacturing will be under laboratory control.

Our building below has been partially constructed and will be completed as quickly as materials become available.

BUY MORE BONDS

DURKEE-MOWER, INC.
LYNN - MASSACHUSETTS

Courtesy Durkee-Mower.

Today the offices are outfitted with modern computers, but the space itself remains the same: paneled throughout in knotty pine with relics of Fluff history mounted on the walls and perched haphazardly on bookcases. Still-life and landscape paintings hang on nearly every wall—skilled watercolors, acrylics, and oils, painted by Allen's brother, Frank. Administrative staff used to occupy both floors of the building, but today, with fewer personnel needed, the company's executives and support teams take up only the first floor. Fred and Allen's offices on the second floor remain mostly empty.

In the factory itself, the production line is almost identical to when the new factory was unveiled in 1950. At that time, modernizing its manufacturing systems provided Durkee-Mower with elegant solutions to a rather fussy, sticky product. Efficiently processing the raw ingredients, preparing the product, and then packing it to ship requires a well-planned production line. For the most part, the new factory's production design has stood the test of time—although, in the bottling area, necessary adjustments have resulted in an astonishing tangle of conveyor belts with jars and boxes coming and going from every direction.

The factory's site along the Boston and Maine Railroad was particularly valuable. A private siding next to the building accommodated up to seven railcars at a time, allowing workers to unload glass jars directly into the factory. The jars were (and still are) then fed via conveyor belt to the first floor in preparation for filling. When rail was the primary shipping mode, roughly three hundred cars visited the factory annually.

Factory mixing room, 1940s.
Courtesy Durkee-Mower.

One major advantage of the new factory was that it allowed Durkee-Mower to switch from the granulated sugar in its traditional Fluff recipe to the new liquid sugar. Liquid sugar removed several processing steps at the refinery, thereby lowering costs. More importantly, liquid sugar could be handled more efficiently inside the factory, making it far less susceptible to contamination and the hazards that come with bulk sugar shipped and stored in individual paper bags. On the side of the building, tanker trucks filled with liquid sugar pump their contents into first-floor tanks capable of holding five thousand gallons. Inside the sugar tanks, ultraviolet light protects the contents from spoiling.

From the storage tanks, the liquid sugar is pumped through stainless steel pipes into a smaller tank on the third floor for mixing and processing. The whipping room—where the real magic happens—draws its supply from this smaller tank. Around the factory, at the occasional leaking pipe joint, little stalactites of clear sugar icicles form.

The third floor's mixing room is an enclosed space where humidity and temperature are tightly controlled to provide a uniform product. Thirteen mixers, each six feet tall, line the space. On one end of the yellow-tiled room a worker opens a spigot to fill a large 140-quart kettle with a mixture of liquid sugars, egg white, and vanillin. Once filled to the correct volume, he pushes the kettle that is resting on a wheeled dolly to one of the two workers overseeing the giant mixers. Hobart Company specially made the mixers, with automatic controls and timing devices, for Durkee-Mower. They are comparable to a beefed-up home mixer with a bulbous machine head rising over a sturdy bowl stand. The worker loads the kettle into the machine, fitting an oversized paddle whip inside it. He clamps a collar around the top of the bowl to enclose any errant spray during the whipping.

With the push of a button, the machine whirls for a magical (and top-secret) amount of time. The thunderous machines preclude easy conversation. All this whipping fills the air with invisible particles, coating the walls and floors with a Fluff film so gummy it pulls on the soles of your shoes. At the end of each day every inch of the room must be meticulously cleaned.

When the liquid is sufficiently beaten and has become a white, sticky foam, the collar is removed and the kettle set down from the mixer. It is then rolled to another worker positioned over a hole in the floor. With one hand gloved in a large, flexible envelope (think of an oversized spatula), the worker tips the kettle down into the opening, scooping all the

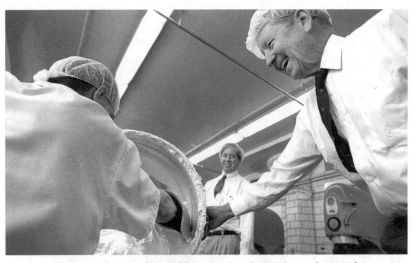

Don Durkee (right) and his son, Jon (center), send vats of
Fluff down a factory chute to then be placed in jars.
(Photo by Suzanne Kreiter/The Boston Globe via Getty Images)

contents into the chute below. Once empty, the kettle is rolled back to the spigot to prepare for another batch.

That opening in the floor allows the warm Fluff to flow directly into a vessel mounted over the filling machine. It's here, in the automation of the filling and packing functions, that the 1950 renovation demonstrated its greatest advancements. To this day, the production line is still impressively speedy. Conveyor belts carry in the sterilized jars and an unscrambler stands them upright in orderly lines under the filling machine. In a single movement, eight jars are filled at once with the fresh Fluff falling from above. A stretched wire levels the tops of any jars that might emerge with a dollop rising above the rim. A worker supervises the activity, using a spatula to top off any under-filled jars or to stop the production line if anything goes awry.

At this point, the movement of production is like a tightly choreographed dance, and anything that throws off the timing puts the entire line in a standstill. The filled jars move on a narrow track to the four-headed capping machine, a merry-go-round contraption that catches each jar and spins it around a central pillar where the red cap is twisted on. One hundred and twenty-five jars take this spin every minute. Just like the freshly whipped Fluff, the caps are stored on the upper floor, sliding down a chute to supply the machine in the packing area.

The jars travel vertically along the track as they make their way single-file into the labeling machine. As gently as an expert tango dancer might guide his partner, each jar is gracefully rotated, twirled, dipped backwards, then pressed with a paper label, the touch of glue like a

Capping glass jars full of Fluff, circa 1940s. *Courtesy Durkee-Mower.*

moist kiss, before it is gently set upright again. Workers pluck any jar with a disheveled label from the line.

There have been some notable changes since the 1950s. Within the packaging section of the production department Durkee-Mower added two stops—one that adheres a plastic tamper-evident security seal under the lid and another to stamp the date and time of production on the lid. (Freshness is guaranteed for six months from manufacture. Dissatisfied customers within this window are eligible for replacements or refunds.)

The biggest change in this area took place in 1964 with the introduction of larger plastic containers. The tubs couldn't fit into the existing filling machine or on the conveyor tracks custom designed for the regular glass jars—so Durkee-Mower simply cut a second hole in the floor of the mixing room and outfitted the plant with another filling machine and packaging line. The mixers, however, can still only meet the demands for one active line at a time, so the factory switches back and forth as required. Some days, kettles are rolled to the hole that feeds the production line for the small jars; on other days, the kettles are slid to the opposite end of the room to carry Fluff to the filling machine for those nifty plastic tubs.

In the far end of the packing area—the oldest part of the Durkee-Mower facility—a loud pneumatic machine folds and seals cardboard boxes with messy squirts of glue. The boxes are then sent ready and open toward the finished jars. Today, the boxes arrive from the new warehouse and enter the packing department from the opposite direction.[1] In order to go where they need to be, they have to double back, which is something of a sight. The boxes travel along an elevated track that ends abruptly, causing the boxes to flip down onto another track below, which is heading in the right direction, toward the bottle picker machine.

At the bottle picker, the jars are automatically arranged above an open box. With the press of a foot lever each box is swiftly filled and sealed. Before this innovation, it took two people one minute to fill seven cases; today, and since 1950, one worker completes ten cases per minute.

---

[1] The warehouse, the newest part of the Durkee-Mower complex, was built in 1963. It sits opposite the administrative offices on Empire Street. Between the two buildings some parking spaces for staff and visitors face a narrow, enclosed corridor that runs parallel to the railway. The corridor connecting the warehouse to the packaging area in the factory is just wide enough for a conveyor belt and walkway.

Boxes of Fluff ready to ship out.
Courtesy Durkee-Mower.

fluff

This cycle of production, called a "row," lasts fifteen to twenty minutes. Because of the attention needed on the production line, those on the factory line have a four minute break before beginning the next row. The factory's line, when operating at peak efficiency, can produce 125 jars a minute, sending five thousand delectable cases of Fluff into the world every day.

With this new manufacturing and packaging process, Durkee-Mower adopted something close to "straight line production." This approach had helped the United States meet the needs of the military in World War II. When confectioners like Durkee-Mower turned portions of their factories over to the war effort, they also gained direct experience with the method. The assembly line, moving ingredients from processing to packing to shipping using a combination of workers and machines, allowed Durkee-Mower to produce Fluff with greater efficiency and lower costs than ever before.

While the factory was celebrated as modern and state-of-the-art in 1950, Durkee-Mower's batch process and plant belied an earlier time. The compressed footprint of the factory, operating on three vertical stories, was ideal for an urban context. But as transportation shifted from railroads to highways, manufacturing was moving away from urban areas. Factory designs were evolving into vast, single-level structures better able to accommodate large, heavy machines, loading docks, and zipping forklifts.

In addition to the factory's vertical design, Durkee-Mower was still using individual mixing machines to manufacture Fluff. By the mid-1950s, nearly all manufacturers were adopting systems of continuous flow production. The next generation of marshmallow cream, as produced by Kraft Foods, would take a more advanced approach. The ingredients are prepared, whipped, extruded, and packaged in a seamless process, resulting in a slightly different, but still comparable, product.

✦

After the transition to the new factory, Durkee-Mower reassigned its existing staff to different tasks in order to keep all its employees. The factory workers in production were now almost exclusively male; the tasks related to packing—formerly women's work—were now mechanized.

Celebrating the Empire Street factory, 1950. *Courtesy Durkee-Mower.*

Common among family-owned businesses, many of the workers at Durkee-Mower remained with the company for decades. For example, Anthony Beatrice, who joined the company in the 1930s (and had presented the gifts on behalf of his fellow workers to the three young men heading off to World War II), was still with the company serving as vice president forty years later. The tradition of promoting from within continues today. Paul Walker, the current vice president of manufacturing, has been with the company for over thirty-five years.

The opening of the completed Empire Street factory was the pinnacle of Fred and Allen's partnership. Though the new building was already in use in 1949, it wasn't until 1950 that the factory was formally dedicated. True to form, a large number of political, industry, and media leaders joined the Durkee-Mower team on a bright June day to celebrate. It was a gathering of friends and colleagues acquired throughout their lives. Among the dignitaries were Lynn Mayor Stuart A. Tarr, chiefs of police and fire from Lynn and Swampscott, presidents of the Lynn and Swampscott Rotary Clubs, members of the Lynn Chamber of Commerce, and the heads of the several local banks. Roy F. Williams of Associated Industries of Massachusetts was there. Karl and the team at the Harry M. Frost agency were present, of course, along with Marjorie Mills, wearing a wonderful hat.

First National Grocery Store, April 1940.
Courtesy American View Company.

The Evolution
of the Supermarket

IN its earliest days, Archibald Query sold Marshmallow Fluff and other confections door-to-door. Archibald's clientele learned of his products directly from the maker himself or possibly through word-of-mouth from other satisfied customers. Archibald's most devoted clients may have placed and picked up orders at his Somerville apartment. When they began their business, Allen and Fred initially took a comparable approach, reaching out directly to potential customers. Their first jubilant sale was a gallon of Fluff delivered directly to the Huntoon House in New Hampshire. But their goal was never to peddle door-to-door. They had aspirations of large-scale food manufacturing, of leveraging the whole-sale trade and the burgeoning industry of distribution that began to grow around another phenomenon: the modern grocery store.

The nineteenth-century equivalent of today's grocery store was the dry goods store. It carried canned goods, dried fruit, pantry staples, such as flour, sugar, and salt, and long-lasting vegetables like onions, potatoes, and carrots. Preserved proteins like salt cod and cured meats were available, too. Customers placed their orders with a clerk who would gather the items from behind the counter, measure them out, and then package the requested quantities. Variety was limited and, of course, the kinds of processed and convenience foods we know today simply did not exist. Other merchants traded perishable items like milk, butter, eggs, bread, fish, and meat. In those days, neighborhood stores operated on credit; accounts were billed and paid periodically, and many retailers delivered. These stores were typically small, two thousand square feet and frequently much less.

Throughout urban neighborhoods, pushcart peddlers offered goods, such as whole fruit, cut flowers, and snacks like candy, roasted nuts, and ice cream. These independent peddlers often provided services as well—knife sharpening and tin and shoe repair, for example. In rural areas, a brick-and-mortar retailer seeking to expand its reach would send out a wagon and offer wares directly to the community. The Great Atlantic & Pacific Tea Company, later known as A&P, was one such store.

Independent food purveyors reflected the areas they served, especially in immigrant enclaves. Brought together by prejudice as much as convenience, newcomers clustered in ethnically defined neighborhoods where they could find bakers, butchers, grocers, and other retailers offering familiar goods and tastes of home. The shopkeepers spoke the language of the neighborhood because they were part of the community themselves.

This model of selling would shift in the early twentieth century with the extraordinary rise of chain stores. Starting in 1900, many retailers—especially those in the grocery trade—began creating networks of shops, carving out dominance in particular regions. A fresh approach to merchandising and a new cash-and-carry model facilitated this shift. Just as domestic scientists were advocating home designs that were less cluttered and dark, retail shops now presented their wares on clearly arranged, easy-to-reach shelves. Even in the smallest shops, wider aisles allowed shoppers to walk unhindered through the store to collect all the items on their lists. Bright lighting and clean floors provided a quick visual assurance that the store's products were of the highest quality.

For the grocers, cash and carry removed the cumbersome expense of delivery trucks and the frustration of uncollected debts. Shopkeepers didn't need to track individual customers and house accounts anymore. Though the upside is clear, this new way of retailing weakened the personal relationships between proprietors and store patrons. But with more cash on hand, savvy grocers could reinvest in their businesses by opening additional locations, typically maintaining the same modest size as they still served immediate neighborhoods. Grocery stores, even today, have distinct, geographically focused customer bases. Before the advent of the automobile and suburban sprawl, the draw for retailers was even smaller.

Chains achieved their economies of scale by centralizing administration and placing large wholesale orders to be distributed to each of their affiliated stores. The chain stores were able to afford and leverage prominent advertising campaigns in local and regional newspapers, luring new customers with the promise of lower prices. Focused on high volume, the immediate return on goods sold at each location provided a fast turnaround of funds, enabling these companies to grow quickly. The transition was explosive. Between 1900 and 1930, the number of companies that operated chain grocery stores increased fortyfold. Within those three short decades, just five companies, with a total of thirty thousand stores between them, accounted for 30 percent of the nation's grocery sales. This trend reflected a broader national movement,

Selling coffee on India Street in Boston, circa 1910.
Courtesy Boston Public Library.

Just a day at the market. Boston, October 1909. Photo by Lewis Wickes Hine. *Courtesy Library of Congress.*

as the economic change driver in this period shifted from a revolution in manufacturing to one of distribution. In New England, three chain stores dominated the market. Coincidentally, just like Marshmallow Fluff, each has close ties to Somerville, Massachusetts.

Stop & Shop got its start in Somerville as the Economy Grocery Store. The Rabinovitz family opened it in 1914 and, in just four years, grew the chain to thirty-two stores. In 1929, the chain reached its peak number of stores with 435 establishments operating throughout the region.

First National Stores, later known as Finast, became one of America's largest grocery chains. It was formed in 1925 through the merger of three companies: O'Keefe's, Inc., John T. Connor Company, and Ginter Company. Emblematic of the industry, Michael O'Keefe, who became president of the newly formed company, was an immigrant

First National grocery store in Somerville. *Courtesy of Historic New England.*

who started as a store clerk, opened his own store, built his own network of stores, and then, through consolidation and partnerships, led this national empire. In 1926, First National centralized its operations in East Somerville to serve its network of seventeen hundred stores with a massive 12-acre, $2 million plant at the junction of Mystic and Middlesex Avenues. (Today, the site would be worth $27 million.) It was developed alongside a new Ford auto assembly plant in a neighborhood that would come to be called Assembly Square. Employing one thousand workers, the complex, as detailed in the *Boston Globe*, included "a great central warehouse, a manufacturing and packing plant, a bakery with a capacity of 1,000,000 loaves of bread weekly, a milk depot, a central garage, and an office building." Its location along the Boston and Maine railroad offered capacity for seventy railcars on two tracks plus additional shared capacity with the Ford plant.

The Great Atlantic & Pacific Tea Company, better known as A&P, started in the late 1800s, expanding from a retail and mail order business based in New York City to become the first American grocery chain. When the company came to Massachusetts, Somerville was A&P's home base. The city housed a major distribution and manufacturing center for the chain, which included a cannery, bakery, and grocery warehouse. Three of the four original buildings remain today just outside of Somerville's Union Square, now converted into housing as the Brickbottom Artist Building.

In two giant leaps, A&P dominated the nation's grocery trade. Starting in 1900, the company grew eightfold in fifteen years, expanding to sixteen hundred stores. The next jump saw A&P grow tenfold in fifteen years, to its peak of sixteen thousand stores in 1930. In that year, A&P stores alone accounted for 10 percent of national grocery purchases.

In the 1930s, Durkee-Mower sales to First National Stores and A&P stores increased by more than 25 percent annually. Durkee-Mower carefully prepared and distributed this glowing report card, detailing sales to each of the chain's distribution warehouses throughout New England— Somerville, Springfield, New Haven, Portland, Providence—and farther away—Albany, Newark, Bronx, Syracuse, Columbus, Indianapolis, Cincinnati, Louisville, Toledo, Detroit, Flint. Orders intended for Somerville for Boston retailers were typically multiples of the orders

fluff

shipped to other centers outside the region. The opportunity to attract even more customers in stores beyond Boston was clear to Allen, who said as much in a letter:

> In my travels and contact with the various units outside of New England, I find the buyers in these units think our sales of Fluff in New England almost unbelievable. I think Fluff has become as popular as it has in New England, and shown a steady gain with the Tea Company as well as with other companies, simply because of the merit of the product, and the very fine cooperation of the companies with whom we do business in New England, in featuring Fluff regularly, calling it to the attention of their customers.

As the chain stores claimed an increasingly large share of America's household food budgets, independently owned grocery stores were falling behind. The independents tried to fight back by forming their own chains to pursue collective purchasing and advertising—such as the Independent Grocers Association (IGA). While still retaining individual ownership, the stores were able to take advantage of more favorable wholesale prices and more effectively compete against the major chains. Overall, however, this was only moderately effective.

For its part, Durkee-Mower tried to remain outside the fray, maintaining relationships with smaller retailers while still courting chains and their immense sales power. But the overall trend concerned economists, community advocates, and politicians. Fearing the long-term impact a loss of market competition would have on consumers, they tried to slow the development of chain stores and level the playing field legislatively. Between 1930 and 1935, a whopping eight hundred measures were introduced at the state and national levels. Most of those efforts failed. President Franklin Roosevelt, worried about escalating prices and seeking to support the millions of households struggling economically, was reluctant to pass fair-trade provisions. In the end, two federal bills did successfully pass. The Robinson-Patman Act of 1936 focused on the terms of wholesale purchases that favored large retail customers, while

158

the Miller-Tydings Act of 1937 addressed the issue of retail pricing.

The Robinson-Patman Act, an anti-price discrimination law, required manufacturers to give the same price terms to all customers. This federal law restricted large retailers from receiving discounts, rebates, and advantageous promotional allowances from their suppliers. While the public could theoretically benefit from lower prices enabled by discount retailers, lawmakers in this case prioritized the protection of small businesses. Wright Patman, the House sponsor of the bill, said, "There are a great many people who feel that if we were to preserve democracy in government, in America, we have got to preserve a democracy in business operation."

Robinson-Patman directly affected business at Durkee-Mower. Durkee-Mower had promotional agreements in place for advertising and store displays with a number of grocery chains. The contracts, in exchange for a financial return on orders, called on the stores to feature Fluff in their printed circulars and in store ads that might appear in local and regional newspapers. Some of these agreements also included advantageous placement on the shelves and signage in the store. Often these promotions were timed for particular events (and peak Fluff interest) such as back-to-school sandwich making or fudge making during the holidays.

In the summer of 1936, Durkee-Mower paid First National Stores its standard 5 percent advertising allowance, but the payment was calculated on orders placed both before and after June 19th, the effective date of the Robinson-Patman Act. The specifics of the new law weren't exactly clear. Suddenly, Durkee-Mower wondered if these advertising allowances were even permitted. Since it was a benefit leveraged by a chain store it could be a violation—though technically,

Circa 1930s.
Courtesy Durkee-Mower.

fluff

any grocer could run a schedule of advertising under a similar agreement with Durkee-Mower. Perhaps it was okay?

Durkee-Mower was nervous. In the small world of New England grocers, if a law had been broken, word would surely get out. A letter seeking clarification was dashed off to Washington D.C., though it was vague enough not to incriminate the company. Meanwhile, a letter was written to First National to chase down the spurious payment. "As we do not wish to place your concern in an embarrassing position, we are asking that our check be returned for correction. ... We may be in line with the Robinson-Patman Bill, and in that case will continue our present contract, making payments as in the past. There is, however, a question as to the texts of our contract and some other incidentals in connection with the bill that we do not understand. ... As the buyer and seller are both liable, we feel that it is the best method of handling the matter and ask for your cooperation."

It took some time but in October of 1936, Durkee-Mower received a letter from the Federal Trade Commission. It clarified that the commission would investigate and pursue possible violations of the law. On other details the letter was neither clear nor reassuring. "The fact that the Commission is required to follow certain formal procedure prescribed in the Act before it can say whether the Act has been violated makes it impractical for the Commission to express informal opinions upon the legal status of matters presented on the basis of hypothetical or ex parte statement of fact."

The Federal Trade Commission did prosecute several large chains and manufacturers for violations, but Durkee-Mower wasn't one of them. While this basic antitrust principle remains in effect today, the law had no effect in halting the steady progress of grocery store chains and the decline of independently owned small shops.

A second law, the Miller-Tydings Act of 1937, clarified the power of manufacturers to set a minimum retail price for their products. This wasn't just to benefit the independent stores being undercut on prices by the chain stores. Manufacturers, concerned that lower prices reflected poorly on the perceived quality of their products, had lobbied for the measure.

To meet this challenge, the chain stores expanded their offerings of store-owned brand products where they had the freedom to determine the price. With this advantage and the opportunity to promote their own proprietary offerings, chain stores took the upper hand, determining the playing field upon which every grocery item would compete. Through these private labels, retailers could easily undercut established brand name items, creating powerful leverage in negotiations with manufacturer seeking to reach the millions of potential customers shopping at America's chain stores.

Store brands weren't new. A&P had taken this approach early on in response to a lawsuit in 1910. Cream of Wheat, the country's largest cereal manufacturer, required all retailers sell its products at a certain set price. A&P, positioning itself as a discount retailer, ignored the manufacturer's requirement and sold the cereal a penny cheaper. Even with the price reduction, through its bulk purchasing power, A&P was still able to make a significant profit. Cream of Wheat responded by cutting off supplies to the retailer. In turn, A&P sued. A federal judge ruled against A&P, stating that Cream of Wheat and other manufacturers had the authority to determine the retail price of their own products and that manufacturers could cease dealing with retailers that failed to comply.

In the wake of the Miller-Tydings Act (and throughout the 1930s, 1940s, and 1950s), store brands expanded as grocery chains and supermarkets grew. Functioning as manufacturer, wholesaler, and retailer, the chains offered the cheapest prices on private-label products, and this undercutting of the competition was the key to their success. Private labels took two tracks. Some emphasized affordability with basic packaging and plain labels, embracing the no-frills ethos, while others followed the style of national brands. On occasion, some store brands gained a reputation for quality, and a loyal following would drive traffic to the store. Store brands, however, were prone to stigma; consumers associated low prices with inferior quality. In general, the strongest store-brand items were those without a perceived difference in quality and those where the savings were significant enough to make up for a small deficit.

A&P, more than other grocery chains of the period, established itself by offering a wide array of store brands, but it wasn't alone. When First National opened its Somerville facility in 1926, manufacturing private-label products was core to its business. Company President

Michael O'Keefe told the *Boston Globe*, "The manufacturing and packing plant will produce a large part of the merchandise for our 1,700 stores that is now bought from manufacturers. We shall continue to handle standard brands as in the past but we shall make candy, ginger ale, salad dressings, etcetera."

The only tool a brand-name product like Marshmallow Fluff had to fight back with was aggressive advertising. Karl Frost maintained his rounds of print and radio advertising for Durkee-Mower. Outreach to home cooks through store appearances and endorsements by media stars like Marjorie Mills continued. Despite private-label marshmallow creams occasionally appearing on the shelves, familiarity and consistent quality kept housewives reaching for Marshmallow Fluff.

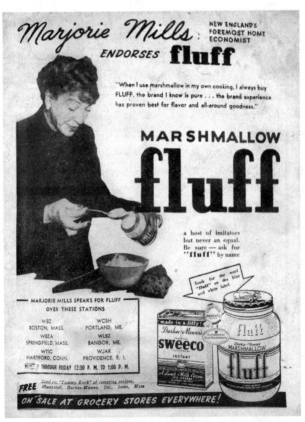

Courtesy Durkee-Mower.

Price mattered, too, of course, and private labels were hard pressed to undercut Fluff pricing. Since its earliest years, Durkee-Mower determined its wholesale prices based on the cost of manufacture rather than a determination of what the market might bear. When the cost of ingredients rose and fell—particularly during the war—the price of Fluff rose and fell, too. Across the century, the price of Marshmallow Fluff has remained shockingly steady and low. Since World War II, Durkee-Mower has increased its price only about once a decade. Today in Massachusetts you'll find a Stop & Shop brand "Marshmallow Crème" for sale for only a couple pennies cheaper than Marshmallow Fluff.

The Miller-Tydings Act has since been amended. In 1951, the Supreme Court determined that manufacturers can only establish minimum prices with the agreement of the retailer, basically adding the "suggested" to the familiar term Manufacturer Suggested Retail Price (MSRP). Retailers can charge a lower price if they so choose. Prices were very much part of the national conversation that year. Through a combination of factors including the Korean War, the American economy was extremely volatile, with food prices dropping about 10 percent in 1949 only to spring back up again in 1950. When voluntary efforts to level fluctuations failed, the Office of Price Stabilization (OPA) created price controls for manufacturers, wholesalers, and retailers, similar to those established around World War II.

Durkee-Mower was no fan of OPA. During World War II, this federal agency prescribed price ceilings and determined the percentage over the net cost for price mark-ups for various categories of manufacturers, wholesalers, and retailers. OPA set the price of many food products, including the wholesale price of Marshmallow Fluff. This meant that, along with coping with the myriad of wartime challenges to make and distribute the product, Durkee-Mower was not allowed to raise its prices to make up for increased manufacturing costs. In 1946, when OPA's restrictions were lifted after the war, Durkee-Mower produced a large flyer that was distributed to its retail partners featuring a cartoon headstone reading "OPA, 1942-1946, RIP." Below it, a character is being squeezed by a vice while another struggles to lift a boulder labeled "Rock Bottom Prices." The poster reads, "In order to RELIEVE the Pressure We MUST RAISE our Prices Accordingly." Effective November 5, 1947, a nine-ounce jar of Fluff was $2.10 per dozen, while an eight-ounce container of Sweeco was $1.90 per dozen.

✦

In the middle of the century, as more Americans took to cars and the suburbs, grocery chains consolidated, operating fewer but increasingly larger stores. This was the birth of the supermarket. In the 1950s, just 5 percent of grocery stores were supermarkets, but they represented roughly half of the total national sales volume.

Supermarkets expanded the traditional grocery store offerings, adding butchers and dairy sections and then delicatessens and bakeries. Piece by piece, supermarkets were taking traditional dry goods stores and all the specialized, small-scale merchants under their umbrella. As cities declined through the 1960s and 1970s, those neighborhood shopping districts crumbled. Once-dominant chains like A&P and First National, which maintained smaller, less profitable urban stores, also began to stumble with this shift. Newer companies and grocery chains that successfully converted to large suburban-style supermarkets took the lead.

Women were no longer the only ones making grocery store choices. Children tagging along on shopping trips gained a stronger voice in what the family ate. Advertising during this period followed suit as youthful audiences watched television shows with commercials targeted specifically at them. Manufacturers of products consumed primarily by young people, like breakfast cereal, cookies, candy, and carbonated beverages, were most effective in competing against store brands. Marshmallow Fluff was part of this trend, successfully taking on strong private label competitors like Solo Marshmallow Creme in the Midwest by targeting the youth market.

These supermarkets were distinctly self-service, with rows of cashier girls at the front and stock boys filling the store shelves. Commodious supermarkets presented a wider variety of products than ever before, giving consumers multiple options in each category. In this environment, retailers and manufacturers alike began to experiment and study the science of product presentation.

As part of its 1954 to 1955 promotion, Durkee-Mower turned to Sunset, a merchandising consultant, for its in-store strategy. Sunset got to work, pushing to expand the brand on the West Coast. "Merchandising Displays for Bigger Sales of Marshmallow Fluff," read the headline in *Grocery News*, a West Coast trade publication from February of 1955. Sunset promoted Fluff with displays at the end of the store aisles at the Pay-Less Grocery and Market in Oakland, California and at the Food Giant Store in Hawthorne, California. These displays were meant to encourage impulse purchases and were situated near the registers. Spaces near the checkout lines with the highest traffic and the longest lingering times were the most valuable.

Fluff on display, 1956.
Courtesy Durkee-Mower.

fluff

In the 1950s, as the variety of grocery store items increased—especially among processed foods—inventory and financial management became more complex. The commonplace metrics we use today were still novel. For example, turnover—the number of times a particular item is sold and replaced on the store shelf—was a revolutionary concept. Discount supermarkets made their money not by maximizing price on individual sales but on volume, earning just a little on each item but selling lots and lots of it.

Bruce Durkee, then serving as vice president of sales and marketing, wrote a column for the trade publication *NEGA* in 1956. "There are very few food merchants who fall for the high profit routine. Turnover is what counts because if the turnover is there so are the profits. Every hour a dead item takes up your valuable shelf space it reduces the profit on that item until finally there is none regardless of what the original mark-up was."

Along with turnover, store items were valuable if they increased the sale of other items in the store. Marshmallow Fluff is nothing if not versatile, explained Bruce, but the key to harnessing such a power was placement:

> The problem of where to place Fluff in the store has confronted many retailers. There is little doubt about most items because their use is fairly limited. However, by actual count there are over fifty items which Fluff is used with. We have actually made tests in stores where Fluff was placed on the shelves next to each of these fifty items and the results were checked as to movement. The three best locations in order were: First: next to peanut butter. Second: next to gelatin desserts. Third: with baking supplies. Check your own location and see where Fluff is. You'd be surprised how little you'll see on the bottom shelves next to the bleaches. Put it next to the peanut butter and watch it move...

Similarly, Sunset also promoted Fluff as a strong product for "related-item selling." Jams, jellies, peanut butter, instant cake mixes, fudge ingredients, ice cream—Fluff could increase related product sales 150 percent when positioned appropriately. Looking for a quick dessert

Young Don (top, center) and Bruce Durkee (bottom, center) get in on the family business at the New England Food Expo, 1950.
Courtesy Durkee-Mower.

combination? The Touca Mart in Burbank, California had the answer; Sunset's display at the end of the aisle put Fluff next to Jell-O.

By the 1980s and 1990s, suburban stores had swelled to one hundred thousand square feet, their vast inventories made possible through computers and digital scanners. Expanding beyond foodstuffs, these super-stores added pharmacies and banking services. Today's mega markets carry a huge variety of items, with the average store offering over forty thousand different products. They are behemoths like Walmart, which claims a quarter of the nation's retail food sector.

Each year, anywhere between eight and ten thousand new products seek space on these vast, but still physically limited, shelves. Manufac-turers who wish to sell through these outlets are exceptionally vulnerable to the retailers' terms—and they can be brutal. One way retailers sort the competition is by demanding payment from manufacturers through slotting fees. In the 1960s, slotting fees were relatively modest. Today, the rates can cost companies from $25,000 to access a regional group of stores to as much as $250,000 for more national coverage. For new-to-market items, stores and manufactures typically make six-month agreements with weekly sales targets. Manufacturers have a strong incentive to promote sales because if those targets aren't met the store takes the product off the shelves and retains the slotting fee.

It's customary, too, for manufactures to pay supermarkets for pro-motion. When stores run advertisements in newspapers or print cir-culars that highlight a particular product, manufacturers pay for that mention. A simple mention runs about $7,000, and a photo can cost as much as $25,000. A sign in the store window announcing a special? There is a fee for that, too. For some products, grocers earn more from the assessment of fees than they do from the retail sales.

Back in its earliest days, Durkee-Mower paid an advertising fee to chain stores (a percentage of the store's overall wholesale purchase), but remarkably, the company claims to have never paid a slotting fee. In the 1960s, when slotting fees began, Fluff already had long-established relationships with New England's grocery chain stores. These com-panies had grown up together. Stores like Demoulas (today known as Market Basket), Stop & Shop, and Big Y already carried Durkee-Mower's product because Durkee-Mower and Fluff were a known quantity;

their customers wanted Marshmallow Fluff. But newer supermarkets don't see a slotting dime from Durkee-Mower, either. Additionally, Durkee-Mower claims to no longer pay for store promotions. Grocers still include Fluff in their promotions and set out displays—reportedly without financial consideration.

How does Durkee-Mower manage to get this preferential treatment? Well, there are only so many marshmallow cream companies to choose from. If the store is carrying this narrow category, Marshmallow Fluff is the go-to brand, especially in the Northeast. Often, the people behind the regional supermarket stores are New Englanders who grew up eating Fluff. They feel a kinship with the brand. Primarily, though, Durkee-Mower makes a compelling case that the company is merely being consistent. It is maintaining a level playing field among all its distribution outlets and treating everyone fairly, from Walmart to the little corner store. They neither pay nor haggle. It's a very yankee approach, letting Durkee-Mower take the moral high road, touting that Fluff consumers pay less because the price isn't padded with a myriad of fees.

Saved by a Sandwich

IN the early 1950s, in this dawn of supermarkets, Durkee-Mower was happily settled into its new facility. After years of making do with a small space and old equipment, the team finally had state-of-the-art tools and enjoyed the pleasures of climate control. A twenty-something Bruce had taken over as director of sales and marketing, and business was good. Not only could the company rely upon its solid customer base in New England, it had opened accounts in Canada for the first time and was looking to realize the untapped potential of markets west of the Mississippi. Durkee-Mower was emboldened. The country, it seemed, contained immense possibilities—but Durkee-Mower's play to increase market share awoke a powerful competitor to those very same opportunities.

Durkee-Mower had witnessed the closure of its local contender, the Emma E. Curtis Company. It was confident that, with the right branding and advertising, it could take others on as well. This goal of coast-to-coast distribution was made easier as several of the company's long-standing regional grocery partners were now national players themselves. The team on hand was at the height of their powers, with Fred Mower on production, Bruce Durkee on sales and marketing, Karl Frost on advertising, and Allen Durkee overseeing it all. It was a confectionery dream team. Looking to corner the marshmallow cream market, Durkee-Mower launched a campaign to establish Fluff as a national brand.

For the campaign, Durkee-Mower associated itself with a partner seemingly way out of its league, the transnational corporation of Nestlé. The centerpiece of the advertising push was a recipe for "Marshmallow Fluff Fudge" made with Fluff, Nestlé's semi-sweet chocolate morsels, evaporated milk, butter, sugar, salt, and vanilla. Fluff fans will recognize the recipe as "Never Fail Fudge."

Never Fail Fudge
Recipe from Durkee-Mower
Makes 2½ pounds

2½ cups sugar
¾ teaspoon salt
½ stick butter or margarine
1 5-ounce can evaporated milk (⅔ cup)
1 jar (7½ ounces) Marshmallow Fluff
¾ teaspoon vanilla
1 12-ounce package semi-sweet chocolate pieces
½ cup chopped walnuts

Grease a 9-inch square baking pan; set aside. In large saucepan combine the first 5 ingredients. Stir over low heat until blended. Increase heat to medium and bring to a full-rolling boil, being careful not to mistake escaping air bubbles for boiling. Boil slowly, stirring constantly for 5 minutes. Remove from heat and stir in vanilla and chocolate until chocolate is melted. Add nuts. Turn into greased pan and cool.

It was a multi-pronged campaign centered on advertisements in seventeen different national magazines with a female market, including *Good Housekeeping, Ladies' Home Journal, Better Living, Everywoman,* and the teenage readers of *American Girl* magazine.[1] Along with an advertisement in *American Girl*, Durkee-Mower produced a double-sided flyer distributed by Fluff brokers to Girl Scouts and other youth clubs. On the front was the *American Girl* cover; on the back was an invitation to try the fudge recipe using Fluff and Nestlé's chocolate chips and a mail-in coupon. Girls were asked to report their results on the simple form and return it to Durkee-Mower for one dollar, an amount sufficient to reimburse the total cost of the required ingredients. The Harry M. Frost advertising agency later explained the strategy: "We're launching this nation-wide promotion for the same reason we are advertising in *American Girl*. We're convinced that youngsters have a strong voice in the food-buying habits of America—and today's young girl is tomorrow's homemaker!"

In regions selling Fluff for the first time, Durkee-Mower focused its efforts on merchandising and education; in regional advertisements it introduced the myriad of uses for marshmallow cream. California was given special merchandising attention; brokers were dispatched to individual stores throughout the state, reporting back on price, stock levels, and presentation at each location. In Long Beach, California, the broker found two rows of Fluff in stock that needed straightening. In Glendale, the jars needed to be pulled forward on the

Courtesy Durkee-Mower.

---

[1]The publication is now defunct and distinct from the contemporary magazine of the same name affiliated with the line of American Girl dolls.

shelf "for better consumer acceptance." In Los Angeles, the store manager was alerted that stock of Fluff was running low.

While the strategy prioritized print promotions, Durkee-Mower didn't forego its relationship with radio, at least not in New England. The company produced a series of advertisements for the 8 a.m. news on the Yankee Network, when it would reach commuters and families at the breakfast table before school. The company was equally interested in promotions that reached the trade. Ingeniously, Durkee-Mower rarely paid for advertisements in those publications. Instead, it leveraged its initial round of consumer-focused ads, letting magazines and radio stations do the work for them. It was here that Karl's long-standing relationships with the media were major assets. These outlets promoted the advertisements Durkee-Mower had run in hopes of enticing other companies to do the same. For example, the Yankee Network ran a quarter-page advertisement in *New England Grocery and Market Magazine* touting the advertising buys for Fluff on morning radio. It was a smart, subtle strategy that put the name of Fluff in front of buyers, all the while underscoring Durkee-Mower's efforts to foster consumer demand.

National magazines typically produced companion periodicals for the retail trade as a way to boost the value of advertising with them, and Fluff worked its way into those as well. Fluff—along with the other advertisers—was included in *Ladies' Home Journal*'s "The Bellringer," a weekly flyer from Roger Bell Food Markets distributed to over 140,000 grocery retailers. *Everywoman* had a monthly flyer for brokers that served as a checklist, organized by category, to record quantities and displays for the individual grocery items advertised in its magazine. Durkee-Mower's Marshmallow Fluff, Royal Instant Pudding, and 7-Minit Fluffy Frosting fell under "Desserts and Frostings." *Better Living*'s companion newsletter didn't mince words with the straightforward title "Better Selling."

As a result of all this work, Durkee-Mower celebrated a record-breaking sales year in 1954. This provided Karl's company yet another opportunity to garner free advertising for its client. It shared the sales news with national magazines and retailers, giving it a back-patting spin. Durkee-Mower's success was not just a result of well-placed

Lt. Governor Sumner Whittier, flanked by Allen (left)
and Fred (right), at one of Durkee-Mower's famous anniversary
parties, 1955. *Courtesy Durkee-Mower.*

advertising, but also of the "cooperative merchandisers in chains, supermarkets, and independents for their promotion of Fluff with allied
products," to stores "becoming more marshmallow creme conscious"
and to "progressive thinking on the part of [store] buyers." The trade
magazines ate it up, echoing the Durkee-Mower announcement in their
publications. For Durkee-Mower, it was another bump of positive notice, and a cost-effective one.

To celebrate the company's anniversary in 1955, Allen and Fred welcomed Massachusetts Lieutenant Governor Sumner Whittier to the
factory to join them for cake and photos and to hoist two flags above
the manufacturing plant: the stars and stripes and another reading "38th
Anniversary." (Remember, anniversary-counting grew muddled after
Durkee-Mower recalled Archibald into its corporate history.) It wasn't as
grand an affair as when it opened the facility five years before, but it got
all the right faces and names in the newspapers. For his part, Whittier,

in the midst of his gubernatorial campaign, gave the company a public shout-out—and more than once, and without much context, joked with the press about gaining a few pounds from eating too much Fluff.

✦

All this publicity led to some big attention in the food industry. *Food Topics* and *Food Field Reporter* selected Durkee-Mower's campaign from among sixteen hundred promotions as their Top Promotion of the Year. Durkee-Mower was among eighty-five companies given recognition and just one of two national advertisers selected from New England.

But there was a downside, too. Fluff had caught the eye of another manufacturer, hungrily scoping out the national sales potential for marshmallow cream. Kraft Foods, the humongous US-based food manufacturer, bared its teeth to take a bite out of the marshmallow cream market.

Clearly, Marshmallow Fluff was on Kraft's radar as it launched its own version in 1957. Kraft was a giant and had incredible advantages—not the least of which were vats of capital to invest in brand new manufacturing facilities. Unlike Marshmallow Fluff, which is whipped in individual batches, Kraft made its marshmallow cream through a highly efficient continuous extrusion process. The different process means that Fluff has a slightly stiffer texture, while Kraft's product has more uniformity in each spoonful. Kraft, new to the marshmallow cream market, played a game of follow-the-leader: It copied Durkee-Mower's color scheme, using a comparable combination of white and sky blue with pops of red. It mimicked the fudge recipe on the label (naming its version Fantasy Fudge and calling for margarine, which it also manufactured). And it threw its ample weight around, buying out (and shutting down) marshmallow cream competitors around the country. It was no surprise that Kraft came calling in Lynn. But Durkee-Mower, due to a sad turn of events, had no intention of selling, especially that year. For the Fluff team, it wasn't just about marshmallow cream anymore.

In August of 1957, Fred was on vacation in Brookfield, New Hampshire. He had a summer home in the small, rural town where he would retreat to relax with his wife, Gladys. Fred's daughter, Joyce, was married now and his only grandson, Peter, had turned five, just the right age for some outdoor adventures. In Brookfield, Fred felt ill and was taken to the closest hospital in nearby Wolfeboro. But there would be no recovery. Frederick Lincoln Mower passed away suddenly at the age of fifty-nine.

So when Kraft approached, Allen had a clear answer. The company that he and his lifelong friend had built would not go quietly. He would fight back with two savvy, ambitious advertising campaigns that made the Never Fail Fudge campaign look like kid stuff.

Following Fred's death, the team was forced to reorganize. Durkee-Mower hired Gerald (Gerry) Kirby as sales manager, and Allen's two sons, thirty-four-year-old Bruce and thirty-two-year-old Don, were given new leadership responsibilities.

Durkee-Mower reassessed the product line. Sweeco sales were faltering under significant competition from national brands, most especially from Nestlé. Durkee-Mower had never been able to properly integrate the promotion of Sweeco into its overall messaging; Sweeco always felt like a tag on. Durkee-Mower began to phase it out, and in 1962, it quietly ended Sweeco production.

The company was now able to focus all its energy on Fluff. Earlier in the 1950s, the company introduced Strawberry Fluff, a simple spin on its central product. This didn't require specialized equipment, sourcing, and packaging like Sweeco. The strawberry flavor used the same production line; it just needed a small shift in the ingredients and a different label loaded into the machine. The jars fit in the same sized boxes and were shelved in the same section of retail stores. Strawberry Fluff would stay.

Durkee-Mower then looked at market trends and reevaluated the growing youth demographic. If kids were the ones influencing grocery purchases, Durkee-Mower's advertising should directly appeal to them. While kids surely liked all the treats made with Fluff (fudge, frostings, and cakes, oh my!), most young people enjoyed their marshmallow cream straight from the jar. Durkee-Mower knew parents would be more inclined to support a steady marshmallow cream habit if it was part of a meal—like a sandwich made with nutritious peanut butter. And even the youngest kid could execute a simple sandwich recipe. And the variations on this modest meal could fuel hours of schoolyard debate: Exactly what kind of bread? Toasted or plain? With or without crusts? Smooth or chunky peanut butter? Add some bananas, raisins, chocolate chips? In a kid's culinary universe there was a broad field for innovation.

Even though Emma Curtis first documented the pairing of her Snowflake Marshmallow Crème with peanut butter (remember the Liberty Sandwich?), Durkee-Mower's Marshmallow Fluff made the combination iconic. The company gave the sandwich a snappy name no one could steal. Henceforth, one and all would call this sandwich "the Fluffernutter."

Richard K. Manoff and his advertising agency staff in New York were responsible for this stroke of genius. Founded in 1956, Manoff's was the first Jewish-owned advertising agency in the country and represented clients like Welch's Grape Juice, Bumble Bee Foods, and cigarette maker Lucky Strike. This 1958 campaign with Durkee-Mower came early in the agency's history. In 1978, the London-based Greers Gross agency bought the Richard K. Manoff Agency, the first in a flurry of British takeovers of American-based advertising firms.

Courtesy Durkee-Mower.

Durkee-Mower rolled out the Fluffernutter campaign with intense fervor. In 1958, the company committed $200,000 ($1.5 million today) for another round of promotion in twelve of the largest US magazines and on radio. Color posters were created for the front windows of grocery stores and for end-of-the-aisle displays. Over a big illustration of a delicious, not-too-oozy sandwich, in big bold red letters was the straightforward text: "Fluffernutter." The text, tilting and uneven on the line, spoke to kids, evoking play and the messiness of childhood. It looked delightful and easy.

Durkee-Mower even commissioned a black-and-white television commercial with a bouncy jingle for the new sandwich:

Oh you need Fluff! Fluff! Fluff!
To make a Fluffernutter!
Marshmallow Fluff
And lots of Peanut Butter.

First you spread, spread, spread
Your bread with Peanut Butter
And Marshmallow Fluff
And have a Fluffernutter.

When you enjoy, 'joy, 'joy
Your Fluff and Peanut Butter
You're glad to have enough
For another Fluffernutter.

The commercial featured a cartoon face hopping on the animated word of "Fluff," then jumping to reveal the name "Fluffernutter." Shots of scooping and spreading a knife full of generically labeled peanut butter and then Marshmallow Fluff on a slice of bread perfectly illustrated the recipe. Bites were magically taken from the completed Fluffernutter before the cartoon face leapt joyfully around a jar of Fluff, its tongue lapping with silly pleasure.

Copycat Kraft was right on Durkee-Mower's heels. It put out its own full-color magazine ads with the headline, "Peanut butter lovers never had it so good. A peanut butter and Marshmallow Cream sandwich made with new Kraft Marshmallow Creme." A freckled, redheaded boy, looking like the popular character Howdy Doody, gives a wide-eyed, closed mouth smile as he holds a sandwich with a half-moon bite taken out of it. But Durkee-Mower had learned its lesson from the Limpert Brothers debacle. This time, it remained one step ahead of the competition. Immediately after the company demonstrated its use, Durkee-Mower trademarked the Fluffernutter name.

In 1964, Durkee-Mower began selling a larger, economy-sized container of Fluff in New England, marketed specifically for families making stacks of Fluffernutters. The campaign was working. Durkee-Mower had succeeded in reaching 70 percent of the US grocery market.

✦

Oddly enough, while it collaborated with other companies over the years, Durkee-Mower never affiliated itself with any specific brand of peanut butter. It's particularly striking because Teddie Peanut Butter is manufactured in Everett—a mere ten miles away from the Durkee-Mower factory. Like Fluff, Teddie Peanut Butter is a New England favorite with a strong national reach. But that's hardly where the parallels end; the history of the Leavitt Corporation, the makers of Teddie Peanut Butter, is strikingly similar to Durkee-Mower's.

The evolution of peanut butter happened almost in parallel with the development of marshmallow cream. Peanuts were first grown in the United States as a commercial crop starting in the early 1800s, mostly as a source of livestock feed. During the Civil War, it was a source of protein for hungry soldiers, and as improvements were made in the cultivation and processing of the legume, whole roasted peanuts were enjoyed as a tasty, portable snack by the end of the nineteenth century. The Inca Indians were making peanut butter in ancient times, but it wasn't until 1895 that Dr. John Harvey Kellogg popularized peanut butter as a source of easy-to-eat protein for his patients, just a year before Fannie Farmer penned her first ode to the wonders of marshmallow cream.

Michael Hintlian founded the Leavitt Corporation in Boston in 1925, just a few years after the start of Durkee-Mower. The Leavitt Corporation is still a family-owned company, now in its third generation. It was founded among the wave of candy companies that launched shortly after World War I. Its early product line included a variety of confections, mixed nuts, and nut butters. The company eventually found its niche specializing in nuts, and today it manufactures and sells nut butters under the Teddie Peanut Butter brand and a variety of whole nuts under the River Queen and Leavitt's Americana Selection brands.

The Leavitt Corporation produces one hundred thousand jars of Teddie each day. Teddie Peanut Butter is even simpler than Marshmallow Fluff in composition, consisting of just ground peanuts with some salt; no sweeteners, oils, or stabilizers. Unlike hyper-processed brands like Jif and Skippy, Teddie Peanut Butter is all natural. The smooth version isn't completely smooth, providing just enough textural bite, while the super chunky version has bits of broken peanuts that, in the opinion of this author, contribute a delightful crunch in a Fluffernutter.

Like Kleenex for facial tissues, Band-Aids for self-adhesive bandages, and Q-tips for little sticks with a wad of cotton on each end, Marshmallow Fluff—thanks to the Fluffernutter tag—triumphed in the name game. For many, Durkee-Mower's Fluff is the only way to describe a marshmallow cream. The Fluffernutter image is so dominant that millions of people remain ignorant of Fluff's many other uses in the kitchen.

Along with the design of its packaging, the Fluffernutter is responsible for Marshmallow Fluff's contemporary brand identity, which communicates a message of childhood innocence, playfulness, and home. Pop culture references abound. In the 1970 pop song "Love You" by The Free Design, the singsong playground tune and lyrics celebrate a blissful youth of running through meadows, skipping, and sunny skies. Among the song's detailed pleasures: "I love forget-me-nots, fluffernutters, sugarpops. I'll hug you and kiss you and love you."

Many companies will pay big bucks to place their products in movies, television shows, and other media outlets, subtly reaching those audiences. But Durkee-Mower, which at this point owns the marshmallow cream market, doesn't need to pursue this because it's simply not necessary. In films and on television, writers and producers use Fluffernutters to establish character. In the gritty HBO prison drama series *Oz*, Cyril, an Irish-American convict suffering from a mental handicap, requests two Fluffernutters as his last meal before execution. The choice highlights his childlike nature, despite his brutal crimes. In

fluff

Courtesy Durkee-Mower.

HBO's *The Sopranos*, Fluff is a connection to home for Christopher, a lieutenant in the New Jersey mob family. After killing the man he believes murdered his father, Christopher visits his alcoholic mother and, longing for his lost childhood, asks her to make him a Fluffernutter. Demonstrative of her inability to emotionally bond with and satisfy her son, she tells him she is out of peanut butter. Christopher leaves dejected, sticking the twenty-dollar bill he robbed from the dead man on her fridge.

Fluff is so distinctly American that in the CBS television series *Madam Secretary*, the main character's children heartily approve of a meal of Fluffernutters upon returning from a trip abroad. "Finally, some normal food!" Fluff also has the power to set the era and communicate a working- or middle-class home. In the Meryl Streep film *The Bridges of Madison County*, for example, the kitchen cabinet is stocked with Fluff in its vintage label. And don't forget the kitsch factor! When John Waters, a bon vivant of all things tacky and wacky, guest starred on the animated television series *The Simpsons*, his character marvels at how the Simpson family's diet embraces all the campiness he loves, right down to Hi-C and Fluffernutters.

Not everyone takes such a wholesome approach to Marshmallow

Fluff. In 1998 on the *Howard Stern* radio show, a syndicated program with a raunchy sense of comedy, a cancer patient's dying wish was to slither in a pool of Fluff with a naked woman. Durkee-Mower declined to ship quantities of its marshmallow cream to the studio, but this didn't stop the shenanigans. Howard Stern fulfilled the man's wish; while on air, he licked Fluff off the body of a female stripper.

✦

Durkee-Mower had no way of knowing then that the Fluffernutter (and Fluff) would endure in such a permanent and prominent way. Back in the mid-1960s, the company had no time to rest on its laurels as it was in the midst of another campaign. This time shelter from Kraft was found under another big company's umbrella: Kellogg's.

Mildred "Millie" Day, a student of home economics at Iowa State University, and culinary expert Malitta Jensen are the unsung heroes of the Rice Krispie Treat. While working in the test kitchen of Kellogg's in Battle Creek, Michigan in 1939, these two women toiled away trying to discover new uses for Kellogg's products. It took the duo two weeks of experiments to refine a recipe for Marshmallow Squares, a combination of puffed rice cereal, melted butter, and melted marshmallows. Though it has had many names, the recipe was featured on cereal boxes as early as 1941 and has remained unchanged.

Durkee-Mower's angle on the Rice Krispie Treat was to substitute regular marshmallows with Marshmallow Fluff. Fluff's smooth texture made it a helpful alternative, eliminating the step of melting the marshmallows. Alas, Durkee-Mower's Rice Krispie Treat campaign wasn't nearly as robust as the Fluffernutter promotion. Indeed, once the campaign ended, Kellogg's retained the Rice Krispie Treat name, while Durkee-Mower continued to promote the same snack—with the generic "crispy rice cereal" listed as an ingredient—under the name of Marshmallow Fluff Treats.

In truth, the Fluffernutter sandwich was the last great marketing strategy employed by Durkee-Mower. The artistry and inventiveness of the late 1950s and 1960s that brought Marshmallow Fluff to glory would not be matched again. The next decades would require a different set of skills from the Durkee-Mower team.

THE
YUMMY
BOOK

Through the decades, Durkee-Mower has produced the Yummy Book,
delivering Fluff-inspired recipes to consumers. *Courtesy Durkee-Mower.*

A New Era for Fluff

DESPITE the unprecedented success of the Fluffernutter, the 1960s was a troubled time for Durkee-Mower. In the background of the company's continued fight against Kraft, Allen Durkee, an active sportsman who loved sailing and golf, battled with Amyotrophic Lateral Sclerosis, most typically known as ALS or Lou Gehrig's disease. In 1968, at the age of seventy-two, his fight ended. Upon his passing, Bruce was named president, with his younger brother, Don, next in command.

There was one bright spot at this time for Durkee-Mower. Kraft lost focus. Kraft wasn't seeing the kinds of profits it wanted and sold off the company that manufactured its marshmallow cream, which was just a tiny part of an exceedingly complex corporation.

In the end, Durkee-Mower's hard work and stamina paid off. The company has emerged triumphant over corporate titan Kraft and other

---

[1]Monolith Kraft Foods is made up of a wide and varied collection of companies that make thousands of everyday items. Tracking the corporate history of Kraft Foods is like trying to unwind a family tree peppered with multiple divorces, remarriages, and a confusing tangle of half-siblings and adoptions. Fundamentally, the Kraft clan is made up of businesses descending from three founders: J.L. Kraft with his processed cheese, C.W. Post of Postum Cereal Company, and Oscar Mayer with his meat business. Within the big related family there's a cast of famous parents like Philip Morris, General Foods,

challengers, claiming 95 percent of the market share in New England and as much as 90 percent in other parts of the country.[1] Despite the new markets, however, Marshmallow Fluff remains primarily a regional product. Turns out yankees love their marshmallow cream—and that folks in other corners of the country just don't eat as much of it. Close to seven million pounds of Fluff are produced each year; 50 percent of it is sold in the Northeast.

What saved Durkee-Mower from Kraft and other challengers was the cold fact that there is relatively little money to be made in marshmallow cream. In the United States, marshmallow products are a $150 million industry, while marshmallow cream is just a fifth of that. Thirty million dollars—put into perspective—is a paltry amount. Compare it to this: in 2013, Americans spent $4 billion on bacon and $14.31 billion just on snacks for the Super Bowl. If marshmallow cream were a more profitable business proposition, if the pie were bigger, Kraft wouldn't have wavered; it simply would have wiped Durkee-Mower off the map, like it did to so many other regional food producers in the 1960s and 1970s. Marshmallow Fluff survived because making marshmallow cream is, in its nature, a modest enterprise.

Given the lack of growth available to this single-product manufacturer, the future wasn't particularly inspiring. And then there is the tricky truth about family-owned businesses. The transition from one generation to the next is perilous; only about 30 percent survive into the second generation and just 10 percent are viable into the third. Durkee-Mower was successfully weathering the storm of corporate power. Marshmallow Fluff remained on store shelves despite the handful of corporations including Kraft, General Foods, and Nestlé that now claimed 80 percent of the packaged foods sales in the United

---

and Nabisco and a huge gaggle of celebrity children like Maxwell House, Miracle Whip, Milk-Bone, Oreo, Ritz, and Jell-O. Even Boston's own Baker's Chocolate got tangled up in this family. While Kraft's is a fascinating tale that includes legendary corporate raids, epic betrayals, and unlikely reconciliations, we'll treat this company the same way it treated its Kraft Marshmallow Creme: reluctantly and in a cursory fashion. Let it suffice that after a rocky relationship, Kraft Marshmallow Creme was banished from the family only to show up again with a different name and a flashy new look as Jet-Puffed Marshmallow Creme.

States. Now, the challenge was from within. Just five years after taking the helm as president, Bruce, who as director of marketing had built a polished, national brand around the product his family had manufactured for half a century, walked away. What happened?

Throughout Durkee-Mower's fifty years, the company's origin story had remained the same: two men, one barrel of sugar, a few tin cans, two spoons, a second-hand Ford, no customers, but plenty of prospects. Back when Durkee-Mower was establishing itself in 1920, Lynn was a city on the rise. When the expanded Durkee-Mower plant opened in 1950, it was part of a spate of notable investments in the community, including the Lynn Memorial City Hall and Auditorium and the Lynn Boys Club. By 1970, however, Lynn, like many other urban communities that had relied on manufacturing, was in a precipitous free fall. The city was struggling with poverty, crime, and blight. Precious few compatriots of Durkee-Mower remained, as many had succumbed to their own battles with corporate competitors. What was left were the vacant buildings and streets littered with remnants of once-vibrant businesses. There was no way to brush off the decline as waves of apocalyptic fires in Lynn (and cities across the country) swept through the mostly abandoned downtown.

Not surprisingly, the economic and class divisions among Durkee-Mower's modest team became more prominent as well. While there had always been a difference between management and staff, the current generation of leadership did not relate to its employees the way Fred and Allen had.

As founders of an ambitious food enterprise during years of growth in the early part of the century, Fred and Allen were participants in a dynamic business world that changed across multiple spheres: revolutions in manufacturing, the effects of war

Celebrating ten million jars of Fluff, circa early 1950s. *Courtesy Durkee-Mower.*

on small businesses, changing government regulations, and the rise of corporate retailers. They had witnessed, participated in, and even cultivated the advent of commercial radio. They were well connected and highly regarded as important civic leaders. Perhaps most fundamentally, they had built something.

After so many years of celebrating the company's anniversary with a cake, the tradition died with Fred. While Bruce and Don had worked at Durkee-Mower for more than twenty years, their participation was simply not part of the company's fabric. After prep school in Vermont and early studies at Dartmouth, Bruce had dropped out of college to go to war before coming to work alongside his father making and selling Marshmallow Fluff. Perhaps Bruce had become disillusioned with his life in some way—numerous letters published in area newspapers illustrate this—but there is also a case to be made that he no longer felt invested in the future of Durkee-Mower.

In 1973, Bruce had enough of Marshmallow Fluff. At the age of fifty-five, he retired and moved to Florida. Though he would remain

The staff of Durkee-Mower outside the Lynn factory, 1945.
Courtesy Durkee-Mower.

titular president of the corporation for a time, Don took over as CEO. Bruce dedicated his days to golf with enough rigor to qualify for the USGA Senior Amateur Championship—twice.

Through the next three decades it was Don who held the company steady. And steady it has remained. In the 1980s, to comply with a new tamper-evident packaging requirement, Durkee-Mower made the necessary addition to the production line. There were a couple notable tweaks to the product itself with the introduction of raspberry-flavored Fluff in 1994 to go along with the existing flavors of strawberry and vanilla. Later, a caramel option was developed exclusively for the European market. Durkee-Mower treats all the specialty flavors as novelties, and Don says he would prefer to phase them out.

In recent years, Durkee-Mower has continued to expand its international markets, making adjustments as necessary. Outside of the United States, Fluff is not identified with kids and Fluffernutters, so Durkee-Mower can market Fluff as it was originally intended: as a helpful ingredient for home cooks. In Japan, for example, tiny recipe booklets looped onto every jar introduce the novel product. In 2015, twenty-five brokers represented Durkee-Mower accounts to grocers and other retailers across the globe.

Jars intended for the international market are wrapped in a different label. The patriotic colors of red, white, and blue are replaced with tones that better communicate the flavors inside the jar. A zigzag bubble circles the message, "The delicious American Marshmallow Spread." These labels, with clunky fonts and odd colors, come across as amateurish and lacking the investment Durkee-Mower once brought to its product design.

Without the threat of Kraft, Durkee-Mower also dialed back its advertising. Kellogg's declined attempts to resurrect the Rice Krispies Treat campaign. Other companies reached out to Fluff to collaborate in marketing, such as Teddie Peanut Butter in the 1990s, but none of these prospective partnerships worked out. The company developed a recipe for Lynne's Cheesecake—attributed to Durkee-Mower's immortal domestic scientist and customer assistant representative, Lynne White. The recipe did not get the kind of robust campaigns that the Fluffernutter and Rice Krispie Treat received in past decades, however.

fluff

―――――――――――――――――――●――――――――――――――――――――

Lynne's Cheesecake

From Durkee-Mower's Yummy Book

SERVES 12-14

24 ounces cream cheese, softened
1 jar (7½ ounces) Marshmallow Fluff
2 eggs
3 tablespoons flour
1 unbaked graham cracker crust or 1 9-ounce ready-to-use crust

Heat oven to 350°F. In large mixing bowl beat cream cheese, Fluff, eggs, and flour until smooth. Pour into pie shell. Bake 45 minutes or just until edges begin to brown.

Turn off heat and let cheesecake cool in oven with the door cracked open for about 1 hour. Remove to wire rack and cool completely. Refrigerate at least 4 hours before serving.

―――――――――――――――――――●――――――――――――――――――――

By the 1990s, Durkee-Mower's print advertising was nearly non-existent, down to just one or two advertisement buys a year. Typically, this ad-buy was an eighth of a page in *Parade*, the circular tucked inside Sunday newspapers nationwide. The placements were timed to coincide with the holidays as a reminder to use Fluff when making fudge. Durkee-Mower maintains a basic website, and not unlike other long-established family-owned food businesses that rely on customer loyalty, it doesn't feel compelled to experiment or invest with social media: No Facebook. No Instagram. No Twitter.

At the start of 2006, Durkee-Mower's primary focus was on licensing opportunities. In the spring, Durkee-Mower announced a partnership with Brigham's Ice Cream for a new ice cream flavor. Established in 1914 in Newton, Massachusetts, Brigham's Ice Cream, like Fluff, was a beloved, local brand. Brigham's business was similarly slowing but the

The New "Yummy Book"

THIRD EDITION

RECIPES MADE WITH

fluff

Durkee-Mower's MARSHMALLOW

fluff

CONTAINS CORN SYRUP, CANE SUGAR, DRIED EGG W...

company still maintained a network of neighborhood restaurants and sold quarts of its ice cream in grocery stores across the region. After several months of development, Brigham's manufactured and distributed a special-edition Fluffernutter Ice Cream, a vanilla ice cream with swirls of peanut butter and Fluff.

That same spring, without engaging with Durkee-Mower, Williams-Sonoma, the upscale kitchen supplies retailer, used the Fluffernutter name to launch a Fluffernutter candy bar, sold in tins from its stores and website. Because it had trademarked the name Fluffernutter in 1961, Durkee-Mower called Williams-Sonoma sharply to task. "They're trying to trade on the nostalgia for the classic Durkee-Mower product without acknowledging our trademark rights. To me, it's a flagrant violation," said attorney Peter Sloane of Ostrolenk, Faber, Gerb & Soffen, a New York firm specializing in intellectual property law.

Up until recently, Durkee-Mower's sales of Marshmallow Fluff were moderate. The factory's production line only operated four days a week during much of the year. The whole company took a break for a couple of weeks during the summer, when the hot, humid days are unfriendly to both Fluff production and sales. In the autumn and early winter (in response to the seasonal uptick in demand), the factory's activity increased to five days a week. One wonders why Durkee-Mower didn't try to jump start activity during that period—to do something, anything, to sell more Fluff. From the outside, increasing sales of its marshmallow cream might sound like smart business—but more Fluff would have required big bucks and dramatic changes that made little fiscal sense. Had the country not realized its health crisis, maybe we wouldn't have heard a peep about Fluff at all.

Courtesy Durkee-Mower.

Why you were born with an instinctive liking for sugar

You get only 4 messages from your sense of taste: sweet, salty, sour, and bitter

The only one of these you liked from the day you were born was *sweet*—the flavor of sugar

This is the way things should be according to what science tells us about sugar

No other food provides us with essential energy so fast

Why do good cooks add sugar to peas? It's a matter of flavor. In taste tests, people say that peas with sugar added taste more like peas. Even soup tastes brighter with a little sugar added. Try it and see.

Sugar helps dieters exercise! The best (and probably the hardest) exercise for dieters is pushing away from the table. Sugar makes it easier by satisfying appetite. No other food does it so fast—with so few calories.

18 CALORIES!
Surprise you that there are only 18 calories in a level teaspoonful of sugar? (Some people have guessed as high as 600.)

No other food satisfies your appetite so fast with so few calories.

All statements in this message apply to both cane and beet sugar.

Selling sugar, 1960. *Image from a Sugar Association, Inc. advertisement.*

Surviving the Nutrition Wars

BY the mid-1970s, domestic science curriculums were fading into non-existence in schools. A common knowledge of nutrition and an appreciation for food-related life skills were subsequently lost. Processed foods and prepared meals, especially fast food, made up the majority of the country's diets. Fewer families gathered at home to share a meal together; children and adults lived increasingly separate lives as the divorce rate rocketed toward its peak in 1980. Heart disease was at an all-time high and cancer was a major, little-understood killer.

Health advocates across the country stepped into action. The last public health revolution at the start of the twentieth century had focused on sanitation and immunization. Now, at the century's close, tackling chronic disease and influencing personal choices around diet and exercise took center stage. The new enemies were fat, salt, and sugar.

Marshmallow Fluff sailed through the attacks on sodium, cholesterol, and saturated fat unscathed. Fluff dodged assaults on specific ingredients like high fructose corn syrup (HFCS). (Remember, Durkee-Mower uses regular corn syrup, a glucose sugar, rather than the more highly refined and twice as sweet HFCS. While HFCS is associated with heart disease, cancer, and liver failure, the glucose sugar in Marshmallow Fluff is free from those dangerous associations.) Marshmallow

fluff

Fluff handily sidestepped many of the campaigns targeted at processed foods, as well. When critics pointed to products on grocery shelves with long lists of unpronounceable chemical ingredients, artificial flavorings, colorings, fillers, stabilizers, and such, Durkee-Mower was able to proclaim Fluff's roots in four simple, traditional ingredients. Fluff wasn't some new, unknown brand made by a corporate food giant that was also in the chemical business; Durkee-Mower was a small, family-owned company right here in New England.

Sugar was Marshmallow Fluff's glaring Achilles' heel.

There's no denying the bare truth that Fluff is primarily sugar, making Durkee-Mower's product an obvious target for any assault on sweets. But the immense power of the sugar industry lobby, comprised of corporate food giants, agricultural entities, and refineries, fiercely protected their interests, providing Marshmallow Fluff with much-needed incidental protection.

In 1870, in the days before granulated sugar at the Boston Sugar Refinery, American per capita sugar consumption averaged fifty pounds annually. By 1900, it had edged up to sixty-five pounds. Today, between the sugar in candy and soft drinks and the hidden sugar in nearly everything else, Americans are eating far, far more. The numbers are hotly contested, but the United States Department of Agriculture (USDA) reported that the annual American per capita consumption of sugar and corn sweeteners topped 150 pounds at the end of the twentieth century.

In the 1970s, the Food and Drug Administration (FDA)—seeking to review the health effects of sugar consumption—found itself hobbled by the Sugar Association and research centers like the International Sugar Research Foundation, which led massive campaigns to undermine any attempts to investigate or regulate sugar.

Chief sugar apologist was Dr. Frederick Stare, founder and head of the Department of Nutrition at the Harvard School of Public Health in Cambridge, Massachusetts. Dubbed "America's nutritionist" in this era, Stare dominated the field, sharing his views in eighteen books, four hundred articles, and *Nutrition Reviews*, a journal he edited for twenty-five years. With major funding from the Sugar Association and corporate food producers like General Foods, Coca-Cola, PepsiCo, Nabisco, Nestlé, and Kellogg's, all of which had a vested interest in favorable

The Sugarletter

A News Bulletin to
the Food Trades from
Sugar Information

NUMBER 5   FEBRUARY 1972

In Brief...

* * *

*"My mother's receipt for plum cake was left
to me, a treasured heirloom: 'Ten pounds flour,
ten pounds sugar, eight pounds butter, twenty-
five pounds currants, two ounces mace, two
ounces nutmeg, one half pint rose water, one
half pint spirits, two pounds citron, ninety eggs.
Make into a paste.' It is hoped the hens are
laying well."*

From an Old Cookbook

SCIENTISTS FIND NEW USES FOR SUGAR AND SUGAR BY-PRODUCTS

A profitable new use has been found for
bagasse, the residue waste from sugar cane after
the juice has been extracted. It's being made
into paper for bank checks. The checks are
said to meet all the quality standards required
of bank note paper. In addition bagasse paper
is easier to use and more uniform in its charac-
teristics than recycled paper.

The First National Bank of Arizona estimates
they will be putting some 120 million bagasse
paper checks in circulation when they complete
their conversion from wood pulp checks. According to the bank, 120 million wood pulp
checks would have required cutting down 4,000
trees. Bagasse and wood pulp paper are comparable in cost.

A new sugar derivative that is held to cut
down tooth decay has been approved by the
National Health and Medical Research Council
of Australia for use as a food additive. It has
also been submitted to the U. S. Food and
Drug Administration for evaluation.

Research has shown that when Anticay, the
name given the new sugar derivative, is added to
processed carbohydrate foods at the rate of one
per cent by weight of the carbohydrate content,
the incidence of tooth decay is significantly
reduced.

The sugar derivative is a white, neutral tasting,
free flowing amorphous powder which has no
noticeable effect on the taste, texture or appearance of foods it is added to. It is also an excellent source of calcium and phosphorus.

Courtesy Durkee-Mower.

outcomes of his research, Stare claimed that food additives were harm-less. He touted the benefits of highly processed, artificially enriched foods like white bread and breakfast cereals, and he celebrated sugar as good for you. Asserting these views before Congress, to federal regulatory agen-cies, and to the public by way of the media, Stare's tainted testimony set national policy and established public attitudes.

In 1974, Stare edited "Sugar in the Diet of Man," a document that for decades provided the crucial evidence to claim that sugar, "mount-ing in importance as a food," was not a "hazard to the public." It was ostensibly a neutral study, but in reality, it was produced on behalf of the Sugar Association. In Stare's report, sugar consumption was deemed not causative of cardiovascular disease and hypoglycemia, and it was just one causal factor among many in tooth decay. Any link to diabetes could not be clearly determined. The finger of guilt for America's health crisis, then only in its nascent stage, was shifted from sugar and pointed toward fat.

Stare wrote his report in anticipation of an FDA ruling that would have been pivotal for the sugar industry. The FDA was evaluating if sugar was "generally recognized as safe," an official agency designation in the evaluation of food additives. Manufacturers were adding sugar to every processed food imaginable, and if the FDA declared sugar as unsafe then sales would have plummeted.

Sugar advocates gained a friend inside the FDA when biochemist George W. Irving, Jr., who had served for two years on the board of the International Sugar Research Foundation, was named as chair of the eleven-member committee. Though groups like the USDA's Carbohy-drate Nutrition Laboratory presented their own findings, citing "abun-dant evidence that sucrose is one of the dietary factors responsible for obesity, diabetes, and heart disease," Stare's report provided a sufficient conflicting opinion to undermine a critical determination by the FDA. The FDA committee was far from ignorant regarding industry influ-ence; the report directly credited the Sugar Association, thanking the group for helpful "information and data." In the end, the FDA conclud-ed that sugar was safe. The Sugar Association celebrated its success with ad campaigns featuring big headlines trumpeting, "Sugar is Safe!"

Americans, by most appearances, willingly went along with the ruse. Doughnuts in break rooms, soda and candy machines in hospital waiting rooms, sugary cereals for kids as "part of a wholesome break-fast"—sugar was given a pass everywhere, even in places where health was otherwise made a priority.

Lobbyists used the findings from the FDA's tainted study to push back against growing public health concerns until challengers, mocked as "sugar haters," fell into silence. With more industry-funded studies, a cloud of scientific disinformation was generated to cast doubt on sugar as the cause of America's ills. Industry proxies like Stare, appointed to leadership positions at the USDA and other watchdog groups, neutral-ized the so-called sugar haters and other powerful enemies.

By the end of the century, the strategy of confusion was so com-plete that even seemingly straightforward facts were impossible to de-termine. For example, there's no commonly accepted estimate of per capita sugar consumption in the United States today. The differences between estimates are not insignificant, ranging from 76 to 170 pounds of sugar per person per year. The fingerprints of the Sugar Association are all over the problem. In 2012, the *New York Times* reported that, not long after sugar trade groups met to discuss the benefit of a lower esti-mate of American sugar consumption and how it might be influenced, the Agriculture Department, tasked with determining this number, revised its methodologies. Overnight and quietly, the agency shaved twenty pounds off its earlier estimate.

Once again, peanut butter came to Fluff's rescue. By sticking so closely with this wholesome spread, Fluff found a safe haven in the overall nutritional makeup of the Fluffernutter. In the 1970s, when Durkee-Mower published the dietary value of Fluff, it maximized its attributes by framing the product within a meal: a Fluffernutter made with enriched white bread and two tablespoons each of Fluff and peanut butter served with eight ounces of whole milk, one carrot, and one apple. Using the USDA's recommended dietary allowances for children six to eight years old, such a meal was highly nutritious, providing 62 percent of the recommended daily allowance for protein, 44 percent of calcium, 27 percent of iron, 54 percent of riboflavin, and a whopping 168 percent of Vitamin A. The fact that Fluff contributed absolutely nothing to the health-positive side of the equation was not under consideration.

fluff

A meal which includes a Fluffernutter made on enriched white bread with 2 tablespoons each of Marshmallow Fluff and peanut butter, an 8 fluid ounce glass of whole milk, 1 carrot and 1 apple furnishes the following percentages of the recommended daily dietary allowances for a 6 to 8 year old child*:

Food energy	32.8%
Protein	62.8%
Calcium	44.8%
Iron	27.0%
Vitamin A	168.5%
Thiamin	30.0%
Riboflavin	54.5%
Niacin	50.7%
Ascorbic Acid	22.5%

(*Figures taken from USDA *Nutritive Value of Foods, Home & Garden Bulletin No. 72,* Revised August, 1970, slightly revised January, 1971)

Courtesy Durkee-Mower.

In 1990, the FDA tried to provide greater consumer clarity with the Nutrition Labeling and Education Act. The legislation required a standard label on all packaged foods showing per-serving nutritional information and establishing some consistency in the meaning of health-related terms like "low fat" and "light." Durkee-Mower, like manufacturers across the country, sent its product off for testing and adjusted its label to include the required new box of information. A serving size of Fluff was set at twelve grams (or two tablespoons) and contained ninety calories. Since the egg whites contribute negligible protein, Fluff is nearly pure carbohydrates. But because the typical serving claims just 5 percent of the total calories in the recommended daily diet, Fluff skated under the radar again as a benign treat.

✦

At the start of the twenty-first century, neither the half-hearted efforts of food manufacturers nor the passionate pleas from nutritionists were making a dent in the nation's health epidemic. Chronic diseases like diabetes and hypertension were responsible for seven of every ten American deaths each year and claimed 86 percent of the nation's health care dollars. Young people were at particular risk. Over the previous thirty years, the prevalence of obesity among children and adolescents ages two to seventeen had tripled, and a third were now overweight or obese.

Low-income youth, who faced higher rates of obesity, were most likely to rely on school-based meals. For this reason, and because of their mandate as the nation's educators, public schools became the front line for officials seeking to address the growing health crisis and to shift America's cultural attitudes toward healthier foods.

Jarrett Barrios, a smart and committed legislator serving as Massachusetts state senator, cared about school lunches as both a politician and a parent. With two children in public school, he wanted to be sure they had healthy food options in their cafeteria. The first Latino and first openly gay man elected to the state senate, Barrios' record of progressive political leadership was notable. Serving the district that covered parts of Boston, Somerville, Cambridge, and other cities to the north, he was integral in working toward the state's landmark recognition of marriage equality. He wrote one of the country's most comprehensive identity theft laws. His advocacy and legislative accomplishments have protected witnesses in state crimes, victims of school bullying, women's health, and those facing foreclosure. This impressive résumé would, however, be overshadowed by a small, well-intended, totally reasonable legislative amendment he filed in the summer of 2006.

In the Cambridge schools, where Barrios' two sons were students, Fluffernutters were an off-menu lunch option every day. If a student didn't like that day's Sloppy Joe, turkey hot dog, or macaroni and cheese, the Fluffernutter was the ever-present alternative to ensure that no child left the cafeteria hungry. Barrios' third grade son, Nathaniel, raised on a healthy diet at home, had heretofore been ignorant of the joys of gooey Fluff and creamy peanut butter sandwiched between slices of soft, white bread. Blissfully, he shared his discovery with his dismayed dad. Apparently, Cambridge schoolchildren were able to order up a Fluffernutter every weekday without their parents ever knowing.

It turns out that in Massachusetts, Fluffernutters solved a perennial challenge for those running federally mandated food programs: it was cheap, it met the USDA's nutritional requirements, it was easy to prepare, and, most importantly, kids would eat it. The fact that neither Fluff nor peanut butter required refrigeration and both resisted spoiling was all the better. While a marshmallow spread otherwise would have been prohibited for offering "minimal nutritional value," the sweetness served as an essential enticement to youngsters to eat protein-rich peanut butter and vitamin-enriched bread.

fluff

A school junk food bill was pending before the state senate, and Barrios used this opportunity to file an amendment that specifically called out Fluffernutters, limiting them within school meal programs to just once a week. What Barrios didn't understand was Massachusetts' rabid attachment to Fluff. He was the son of Cuban-American parents, had grown up in Florida, and only moved to Massachusetts as a young adult to study at Harvard. How could he have known that the white, super-sticky marshmallow spread was part of the state's DNA?

Barrios' Fluff amendment sparked conversation among legislators, their aides, reporters, and the general public. They shared stories about Marshmallow Fluff, how they enjoyed it as kids, and wondered whether they still had a jar at home. And it got people to start acting like kids themselves. State House reporters had something to lighten up their usually dry articles. Political blogs ran with the silliness, including one that invented a "Barrios Fluff Advisory System," based on the terror-alert system. State Representative Kathi-Anne Reinstein, whose district included Fluff-producing Lynn, engaged in some good-natured ribbing when she filed a bill, citing the "legacy of this local delicacy," to declare the Fluffernutter the state's official sandwich.

The story of the Fluffernutter kerfuffle took off like wildfire. Judging by the vitriol on talk radio, it was, quite literally, like Senator Barrios had ripped candy from a baby. For many, it was a demonstration of government do-gooders running amok with a beloved New England delight, telling people what they could and couldn't do. Print and television reports poked fun at the absurdity that was taking place in the Massachusetts State House. National late-night and morning television hosts like Jay Leno, Regis Philbin, and Kelly Ripa joked about the feud. All over the world, from Japan to New Zealand, media outlets picked up the story.

Barrios' office was overwhelmed with angry and mocking calls and letters, even death threats. Aide Colin Durrant was left with the unenviable task of representing the embattled senator, who needed to demonstrate that he was in on the joke while continuing to rationally advocate for changes in food programs in schools. "[Senator Barrios] loves Fluff as much as the next legislator," Durrant told the *Associated Press*. "He has signed on to cosponsor Representative Reinstein's bill but still believes

Fluff can't be a substitute for a healthy and nutritious meal."

The team at Durkee-Mower tried to keep their heads down amidst the pandemonium. Don told the media, "Like most people, I think it is a little frivolous to bring it to the attention of our governing bodies. … I think obesity is a problem, but I don't think it can be legislated."[1]

Suddenly, the typically sleepy MarshmallowFluff.com website was blowing up with orders. On Empire Street, the secretary's office reportedly "looked like a warehouse," with cases prepared for shipment piling up and taking over. The outpouring of appreciation and interest might have turned a promotion-hungry company smug or opportunistic, but Durkee-Mower remained nonplussed. Dan Quirk, Durkee-Mower's vice president of sales and marketing, said at the time, "We weren't that concerned because we don't push it as a health food. … But, naturally, we don't care for negative publicity." He went on, "We had our moment in the sun. We're now hoping it all just goes away."

No matter where you fall in the Great Fluffernutter debate of 2006, and regardless of your affection for this quirky product, Durkee-Mower's sentiment likely comes across as illogical. It's vaguely un-American that a business shrinks from this kind of adoration and publicity gold. As I came to understand this paradox, I finally uncovered the lessons hidden within the Marshmallow Fluff story.

---

[1] Senator Barrios' so-called Fluffernutter amendment quietly disappeared at the end of the legislative session. Within a year and before the end of his term, Senator Barrios resigned. While his work in the public health arena continues, he turned his back on elected office.

Time to make the Fluff.
Courtesy Shelby Larsson.

The Catalytic Power of Fluff
(Or the importance of sticking to things)

WHAT makes something iconic?

The second half of Durkee-Mower's history provides a stark contrast to its early decades, when innovation and ambition buoyed the company's success. For more than half its history, the company's survival required steadfast consistency. During Don's decades of leadership, it has been his dogged approach—whipping up five thousand cases of Fluff each day, year after year after year, without fanfare—that has allowed Durkee-Mower to persevere. Meanwhile, everything that surrounds Durkee-Mower and Marshmallow Fluff has changed. As the once-thriving manufacturing city of Lynn stumbled, the company soldiered on. It has prevailed over competitors and the tumult of changing tastes. And Don himself has carried on despite personal losses and the sometimes lonely, dispiriting days of repetition. Almost completely un-altered, Marshmallow Fluff—the company's sole remaining product—has weathered the vagaries of time, same as it ever was.

At the close of the twentieth century, the machinery was still in working order, but Durkee-Mower was weary. Somewhat understand-ably, Don and his son, Jon, were downright surprised by the virulent response to Senator Barrios' Fluffernutter amendment. (They weren't alone, of course. Barrios was equally floored.) But to the Durkee-Mower crew, who should have known the beguiling charm of the confection best of all, their myopic response was as though they had been sleep-walking for the past forty years. Had they looked out the windows of the Lynn factory they might have noticed the expressions of heartfelt affection for their Marshmallow Fluff springing up everywhere.

The Fluff renaissance was first apparent on the menus of restaurants in New England and beyond. Young, inventive chefs created playful desserts that recalled childhood. Bringing Fluff back into the kitchen, these imaginative offerings took a fresh approach to old classics, like grown-up whoopee pies, trendy cupcakes with marshmallow frostings, and a brûlée of Fluff upon an artfully arranged plate.

Concurrently, a new generation of upstart food entrepreneurs was beginning to re-energize American cities, including Fluff's hometowns of Somerville and Lynn. Not unlike Archibald Query and Emma and Amory Curtis a century ago, they experimented in their apartments and shared commercial kitchens, making their own marshmallows and marshmallow creams. They embraced new flavors like green tea, lemon, bourbon, and spicy cinnamon and sold their hand-cut marshmallows at open-air markets, online, and at the new independently owned grocery shops slowly returning to urban neighborhoods. These artisan makers elevated the reputation of what was often considered inexpensive, even tawdry, forgettable pillows of sugar. They did wonders for its smooth, spreadable cousin, marshmallow cream, as well.

Starting around 2000, a number of artists seeking to communicate complex messages about home, food, childhood, and America found a vehicle in Fluff's stout jar, unchanging label, and patriotic red, white, and blue color scheme. Fluff was on its way to becoming something akin to Warhol's Campbell Soup Cans. Crafty Fluff fans found inspiration too, making and selling jewelry, magnets, stickers, and trinkets. Despite Durkee-Mower's ostensible complacency, Fluff kept showing up in the most interesting places. Two NASA astronauts with Massachusetts ties, Sunita "Suni" Williams and Richard Linnehan, each packed jars of Fluff to share Fluffernutters with their colleagues while on board the International Space Station.[1]

---

[1] The stickiness of Fluff and peanut butter makes the Fluffernutter a perfect treat in weightless atmosphere. Because breadcrumbs float and cause a mess, tortillas provided an excellent bread substitute for the out-of-this-world version.

Chocolate had undergone a comparable reversal of fortune. Just like marshmallows, chocolate in the 1960s and 1970s fell into disrepute. Walter Lowney's bonbons and other chocolates of the previous century were once an affordable luxury, hand-dipped and made with high quality ingredients; but after decades of corporate cutting, "fancy" chocolates were no longer fancy. Boxed chocolates had become the mainstay of dime stores, holiday impulse gifts that said, "Oops, I almost forgot," more than they said, "I can't stop thinking about you." The chocolate itself was waxy and stale tasting. The fillings were an assortment of pasty, artificially flavored goo. Hardly luxurious. What's more, candy had been promoted as quick and cheap sustenance for folks on the go for so long, it was hard to convince people that it was suddenly a decadent treat to be savored.

Godiva changed all that in the 1980s, attaching its fine chocolates to the omnipresent images of glamour and extravagance that marked the decade. Full-page ads in high-end magazines presented carefully selected chocolates like fine jewels. With stores in luxury malls, gold foil presentation boxes, and a logo modeled on a family crest, Godiva remade chocolate. It was no longer plebian fodder, but elegant and classy. Almost single handedly, Godiva boosted the American appetite for chocolate; per capita consumption leapt by two and half pounds between 1980 and 1985.

While the evolution of marshmallows (and marshmallow cream) isn't so blatantly class-based, interest has broadened and sales have increased. Between 2010 and 2014 the inclusion of marshmallows on restaurant menus increased by 63 percent and the demand is evident on company bottom lines too, with snacks and desserts that include marshmallows resulting in 29 percent higher profits. Marshmallow products might never achieve chocolate-like status, but the confectionery category isn't entirely forgotten either.

But perhaps most telling is that, unlike Godiva Chocolate, Marshmallow Fluff has never reinvented itself. Since 1988, Durkee-Mower has not invested any significant money in advertising or promotion; the same Never Fail Fudge recipe still graces the label on the jar, and there is no grand plan to increase market share. With the exception of liquid sugar, the recipe has remained the same since it was first whipped up in Archibald Query's kitchen. Its popularity may fluctuate, but Fluff's constancy may be its most vital feature.

Fluff sales have increased over the past ten years. In recent years, Durkee-Mower has been operating year round, even increasing its production line to six days a week in the fall. (One imagines that this has as much to do with the growing interest in marshmallows as it does the growing interest in the *What the Fluff?* festival.) When asked about this, Don Durkee seemed bemused, "Our sales have gone up steadily every year the past few years. We're not doing anything different. I have no idea why people are buying more Fluff."

Marshmallow Fluff has, through its longevity, transcended time, forging a personal connection with each successive generation. No matter their age, everyone relates Fluff to their own childhood. Anyone who has ever stuck a finger into a jar of Fluff can claim it as their own. For the chefs, artisan foodies, astronauts, artists, and crafters—not to mention a whole new generation of customers—Fluff embodies the comforts of home, both in the familial sense as well as the cultural.

While the name might beg an ironic approach, Marshmallow Fluff is nothing but sincere. The packaging, recipes, advertising, and the Durkee-Mower company itself are without guile. Indeed, the product feels like it is stuck in a time warp, forever harkening back to its heyday of postwar enthusiasm and economic growth. Fluff is utterly optimistic. It recalls the birth of modern consumerism and all those jingles of radio's burgeoning years. The singular irony is that Durkee-Mower's commitment to the status quo has led the product to this enviable cultural status.

✦

Back in 2006, when I proposed the festival to honor Archibald Query and his invention of Marshmallow Fluff, I wasn't aware of the marshmallow cream zeitgeist. I was as surprised as everyone else when Senator Barrios' Fluffernutter amendment provided our little neighborhood party with a publicity tidal wave to ride.

Through the *What the Fluff?* festival I attempted to poke fun at the cultural obsession with all things new and trendy. I suppose it was my small protest from the depths of boot-strapping Union Square against the prosperous start-ups in Kendall Square—an ornery fist-shake at the "disruptors" and "innovators" riding roughshod over folks like me just trying to get by and get their jobs done. Ironically, by focusing on the celebration of Archibald Query's invention of Marshmallow Fluff, I was revealing myself as a hypocrite. Shining such a bright spotlight on this tiny sliver of the Fluff story, I was wiping out the entire history of Durkee-Mower and Lynn and all the years of hard work embodied in this century-old product.

Today, I know so much more about Marshmallow Fluff and the people who made it—and the story of Fluff is really the story of America in a jar. I learned how Fred met Archibald on the shop floor of Walter Lowney's factory, how Fred, his dear friend Allen, and their buddies collaborated to build a successful company. I met those who inspired their ambitions, like Emma and Amory Curtis, as well their corporate foils. I discovered key Fluff allies like publicist Karl Frost and media maven Marjorie Mills. I marveled at the luck of happenstance—of being in the right place at the right time—and the agility to harness cultural shifts such as the rise of the supermarket and domestic marketing. I witnessed Durkee-Mower's heady moments, pioneering radio and building a new factory, and the difficult days when it was a challenge just to get Fluff made. I witnessed moments of crisis, facing down the Limpert Brothers and Kraft, when the company's very existence was on the line.

I've seen the essential contributions at each stage of the Marshmallow Fluff story—the unique gifts granted by those who start, those who build, and those who sustain. I see in this lessons for the cities of Somerville and Lynn and other communities trying to balance new eras of prosperity and displacement.

In my work, I often look at the merits and pitfalls of running after trends: sometimes you embrace the new—like radio, sweet milk cocoa, liquid sugar—and sometimes you just hold tight to what works. Durkee-Mower remained rooted in the community that produced it, never succumbing to greed or overconfidence, always staying the course. Its reward for this is a product that has achieved an unintended symbolism. Sure, Marshmallow Fluff tastes good, but what it represents may be the sweetest part about it.

© *Union Square Main Streets.*

fluff

Ultimately, the story of Marshmallow Fluff reminds me of the immeasurable, often-overlooked value of those who carry on, those who maintain their companies and neighborhoods through "ordinary" times, when the promise of change is distant, when there's just the selfless work of the daily grind in order to make it to tomorrow. In Lynn, Somerville, and countless other hard-luck cities now turning a corner toward new growth, it's important to remember those who kept showing up, even when there was little rational reason to do so. Marshmallow Fluff exists today—and neighborhoods like Union Square have character today—because there are dogged people like Don Durkee coming to work to whip up yet another jar of Fluff.

Courtesy Durkee-Mower.

The Archibald

*By Paulo Pereira, general manager and
beverage director at Brass Union*

1½ ounces marshmallow vodka
¾ ounce Jägermeister
½ ounce coffee liqueur
1 ounce Fluff-coconut milk (directions follow)*

Add all ingredients to a shaker, fill with ice, and shake vigorously for 10 seconds. Strain over fresh ice into a rocks glass. Garnish with mini marshmallows.

To make Fluff-coconut milk: In a high-powered blender, add equal parts coconut milk and Fluff. Blend until it's liquefied.

fluff LABEL TIMELINE

Over the years, Durkee-Mower has modified Fluff's package and design to meet expectations of the marketplace. It could be argued that popular affection for Fluff comes as much from its portly jar, retro spoon, and colors befitting its wholesome American pedigree as it does from the sweet confection inside.

It's good for children!

For much of its history, Fluff (like other marshmallow creams) was sold in cans with a screw-top metal lid. For a period in the 1930s, Durkee-Mower changed to a flip-top lid, which Fluff devotees gently opened with a coin or spoon handle.

In the 1920s, the label was almost Victorian in style. Against a background of light blue stripes, "Durkee-Mower's" appeared in red script. Beneath, "Marshmallow Fluff" was printed in varying hues of blue and white. A colorful fruit parfait topped with Fluff and a bright red cherry was flanked by the words: "An Excellent Cream for Frostings, Sauces, Fillings, Meringue," and "An Exquisite Cream Fluff for Fudge, Hot Chocolate, Soda Fountain Delicacies."

It blends and spreads!

In self-service grocery stores, manufacturers like Durkee-Mower relied on the silent salesman: packaging. The container and label needed to communicate essential information about the contents while also implying the company's impeccable values, establishing a relationship of trust.

Late in the 1920s, the Fluff label was redesigned to appear more modern. The color scheme remained predominantly light blue and white with dark blue accents, but the word "Fluff" took center stage. The tops of Marshmallow Fluff tins were unpainted and embossed with, "The original Marshmallow FLUFF," and the catchphrase: "It blends and spreads easier."

It is the artwork of Nash and Petrucci that graces the Fluff label today—even on those modern plastic 5-pound tubs. Plastic containers were introduced in 1964, as the economy-size container came to the rescue of families hungry for Fluffernutters morning, noon, and night.

One heaping spoon!

With tin needed for military uses during World War II, Durkee-Mower converted to a glass jar and never looked back. The label, however, didn't significantly change until the mid-1950s as part of nation-wide marketing push. This iconic design benefited from the talents of two artists.

James Harley Nash was responsible for the lettering, creating the distinctive style of the word "fluff" we recognize today. Based in New York, Nash made a splash in the design world early in his career. He was still a student in 1915 when his "Made in the USA" design was selected out of 120,000 entries for best national trademark. He went on to design and influence some of the most iconic brands in America. Nash modernized that kindly Quaker Oats man and created the Socony Flying Red Horse that became the enduring logo for Mobil gasoline. Nash was even part of the effort to redesign the packaging of military K-rations during World War II.

The other lasting design element was that heaping spoon, created by Medford-native Sam Petrucci. Petrucci was also behind the merchandising art for GI Joe, including Hasbro's 1966 "Action Soldiers of the World" line. Petrucci illustrated Mr. Potato Head's packaging as well as packaging for Charleston Chew, Ocean Spray, Polaroid, and Prince Spaghetti. The Lassie lunchbox he designed is preserved at the Smithsonian Institute.

ACKNOWLEDGMENTS

A BIG THANK YOU to the team from Union Park Press, who transformed my manuscript and a mish-mash of images into the honest-to-goodness, real-life book you have in your hands. A special thank you to Nicole Vecchiotti for her leadership, Deepa Chungi for her gentle and creative editing, Shelby Larsson for her promotional prowess, and Caitlin Dow for her sharp eyes and hard work.

I'm grateful for the cooperation of the people of Durkee-Mower with specific thanks to Don Durkee, Jon Durkee, and Dan Quirk.

I'm indebted to the countless people who carefully collect, catalog, and preserve local history. A special thank you to Jeff Myers and Jeremy Spindler of The Boston Candy Museum at Spindler Confections, radio historian Donna Halper, Andy Todesco of the Mansfield Historical Society, and the staff of the public libraries in Somerville, Melrose, Swampscott, Lynn, and Medford. A big hug to all the folks at the Somerville Museum, especially Evelyn Battinelli, David Guss, and Michael O'Connell, and to Nicole Breault and Britt Bowen at the Lynn Museum.

Over the years as I organized the Fluff Festival, the energetic, fun-loving people of Somerville strengthened my connection with this somewhat-silly confection. If the annual event hadn't become such an inescapable phenomenon, I wouldn't now be so thoroughly stuck on Fluff. While I'm no longer running the happening, my affection for this exceptional community is eternal.

My parents and big, inventive, energetic family are a constant source of inspiration and sustenance. Special Fluff appreciation for my brother, Mike, for inventing the Tuna Fluffer and proving that Somervillians really will eat anything paired with Marshmallow Fluff.

I'm indebted to friends who patiently listened to my enthusiastic recital of Fluff-related trivia and helped me to puzzle through how to tell this story. Those who endured with the greatest aplomb were MaryCat Chaikin, Wayne Strattman, Shannon McDonough, and Lisa Horowitz. Thank you, Ingrid Lysgaard, for going the extra mile and serving as my gentle reader.

Finally, I'm ever grateful for the two men in my life. Thank you, Chris Dewing, for being such a source of pride. And much love for my husband, Scott Loring, for your unwavering belief in me.

NOTES ON SOURCES

Along with original source material, including interviews with members of the Durkee and Query families, the Durkee-Mower archives, contemporary and historical newspapers, and other print publications, my research relied on the following books:

Brenner, Joël Glenn, *The Emperors of Chocolate: Inside the Secret World of Hershey and Mars*. Toronto: Random House, 1999.

Blackford, Mansel G., *A History of Small Business in America*, Second Edition. Chapel Hill: The University of North Carolina Press, 2003.

Cushing, Elizabeth Hope, ed., *No Race of Imitators: Lynn and Her People, an Anthology*. Lynn: The Lynn Historical Society, 1992.

Goldstein, Dara, ed., *The Oxford Companion to Sugar and Sweets*. New York: Oxford University Press, 2015.

Grover, Kathryn, *The Lynn Album II: A Pictorial History*. Lynn: The Lynn Historical Society. 1996.

Halper, Donna L., *Boston Radio 1920-2010*. Charleston: Arcadia Publishing, 2011

Halper, Donna L. *Invisible Stars: A Social History of Women in American Broadcasting*, Second Edition. New York: M.E. Sharpe, 2014.

Kawash, Samira, *Candy: A Century of Panic and Pleasure*. New York: Faber and Faber, 2013.

Leavitt, Sarah A., *From Catharine Beecher to Martha Stewart: A Cultural History of Domestic Advice*. Chapel Hill: University of North Carolina Press, 2002.

Liesener, Katie, "Marshmallow Fluff." *Gastronomica: The Journal of Food and Culture*, Spring 2009.

Morris, Dee and Dora St. Martin, *Somerville: A Brief History*. Charleston: The History Press, 2008.

Paul, Ellen Frankel, Fred D. Miller, Jr, Jeffrey Paul, ed. Freedom of Speech. Cambridge: Cambridge University Press, 2004.

Puleo, Stephen, *Dark Tide: The Great Boston Molasses Flood of 1919*. Boston: Beacon Press, 2003.

Stadelman, William J., Debbie Newkirk, Lynne Newby, *Egg Science and Technology*, Fourth Edition. RC Press, 1995.

Stage, Sarah, and Virginia B. Vincenti, ed., *Rethinking Home Economics: Women and the History of a Profession*. Ithaca: Cornell University Press, 1997.

Stiegart, Kyle E. and Dong Hwan Kim, ed. *Structural Changes in Food Retailing.* Madison: University of Wisconsin, Food System Research Group, 2009

Untemeyer, Louis, *A Century of Candymaking 1847-1947: The story of the origin and growth of New England Confectionery Company which parallels that of the candy industry in America.* Boston: The Barta Press, 1947.

Voss, Kimberly Wilmot, *The Food Section: Newspaper Women and the Culinary Community.* Lanham: Rowman & Littlefield, 2014.

Wyman, Carolyn, *The Great American Chocolate Chip Cookie Book.* Countryman Press, 2013.

Lynn: One Hundred Years a City. Lynn Public Library and the Lynn Historical Society, 1950.

INDEX

fluff

ABOUT THE AUTHOR

MIMI GRANEY is the founder of *What the Fluff?*, a festival celebrating Marshmallow Fluff that draws thousands annually. Her work in neighborhood economic development takes her to communities across Massachusetts where she focuses on creative industries and food-based businesses. Her favorite way to enjoy Marshmallow Fluff is by the melting spoonful in a mug of hot chocolate.